THE
BROTHERS
HOGAN

Jacque Hogan Towery

THE
BROTHERS
HOGAN

A FORT WORTH HISTORY

Jacqueline Hogan Towery
Robert Lindley Towery
Peter Barbour

TCU Press
Fort Worth, Texas

Library of Congress Cataloging-in-Publication Data

Towery, Jacqueline Hogan, 1933- author.
 The brothers Hogan : a Fort Worth history / Jacqueline Hogan Towery
and Robert Lindley Towery and Peter Barbour.
    pages cm
 Includes bibliographical references.
 ISBN 978-0-87565-596-3 (alk. paper)
 1. Hogan, Ben, 1912-1997. 2. Hogan, Royal, 1909-1996. 3. Fort
Worth (Tex.)--Biography. 4. Golfers--Texas--Fort Worth--Biography.
5. Businessmen--Texas--Fort Worth--Biography. 6. Hogan family. I.
Towery, Jacqueline Hogan, 1933- author. II. Towery, Robert, 1932-2010
author. III. Title.

 F394.F7B37 2014
 338.092'2--dc23
 [B]

                               2013042130

TCU Press
P.O. Box 298300
Fort Worth, Texas 76129
817.257.7822
www.prs.tcu.edu

To order books: 1.800.826.8911

Designed by Bill Brammer
www.fusion29.com

CONTENTS

ACKNOWLEDGMENTS

The authors are grateful to the following people for their invaluable contributions:

Jimmy and Claudia Atkinson
Pucker Barse
Don Bassham
Joy Crowder Begley
Lindy and Geno Boxshardt
Dan Buford
Mary Garcia Christian
Ray Coleman
Colonial Country Club
Earl and Corrine Collins
Dr. David Corley, Jr.
Dayna Corley
David Corley, Sr.
Jeddy Corley
Scott Corpening
Eddy Deems
Bill Denkins
Rita Eatherly
Don Gault
Glen Garden Country Club
Elizabeth Hudson
Dan Jenkins
Jody Lancarte
Lanny Lancarte
Mike and Donna Leman
Marty Leonard
Leonard Store Museum
Darrell Lester
Pat Martin

Don Matheson
Melvin May
Charlie Moncrief
Tex Moncrief
Jane Smith Monell
Cecil Morgan
Dr. Jim Murphy
Joe Peters
Dennis Roberson
Marianne Hannon Schofield
Wally Schmuck
Shady Oaks Country Club
Mike Ship
Chuck Spence
Johnny Thomas
Jerre Todd
Bill West
George Wilkes
Lindsey Wilkes
Billy Wood
Mike Wright
Larry and Murlyn Zeske
Peter Barbour's research
  assistant: Lory Donatt
An extra special thank you
  to Max Swafford
And all of the hard workers
  at TCU Press

INTRODUCTION

Robert Towery was the original author of this unique biography. Sadly, he passed away on October 29, 2010, before he was able to complete his vision. I had known Robert since I was eleven years old, when he drafted my brother, Larry, into the Babe Ruth League baseball team he coached in the 1960s. In April of 2010, I had the opportunity to discuss the project with Robert and Jacque during one of their visits to Austin, when Robert first told me about the book he had started based on Jacque's unique perspective on the Hogan family. He had done years of research and had taped interviews from a myriad of individuals who had significant relationships with the family. He said he had written about seven chapters and had outlined the rest of the book. At the time, I offered my services as a proofreader/editor, if he required them, and he said, "I might take you up on that."

Soon after our April meeting, Robert was diagnosed with pancreatic cancer and passed away within six months. I didn't hear about the project again until Jacque called me about a year and a half after Robert died. She told me that during the last days of his life, she promised Robert to get his book published. Jacque asked me if I would help her finish the work her late husband had started. I was honored to be a part of *The Brothers Hogan* and I hope what Jacque and I completed honors the memory of its creator, Robert Towery.

The following is the original introduction Robert wrote for the book.

I am married to Jacqueline Hogan Towery, the daughter of Royal Hogan and the niece of Ben Hogan. For years people have suggested that Jacque write a book about the Hogan family, but my wife is not the type to spend hour upon hour writing down the stories of her life. However, this narrative must be told and published, so the task has been handed to me.

Jacque and I were both born in Fort Worth, Texas, and attended public school at R. L. Paschal High School, where we met and were classmates. When we graduated, she went to Southern Methodist University in Dallas, and I went to Austin to play baseball at the University of Texas. We did not see each other again for forty years.

I graduated from the University of Texas School of Law in 1958, went to work for the District Attorney of Travis County, and stayed in Austin for forty years. Jacque married an SMU graduate from Corsicana, spent several years moving around with her husband, who was in the Air Force, returned to Fort Worth, and raised a family.

When our class of '51 held a fortieth year reunion in 1991, Jacque and I attended and saw each other for the first time since we were seniors in high school. After raising four children, she was again a single lady, and I was in the process of a divorce. We sat together at the reunion dinner and renewed our friendship. We enjoyed each other's company so much that we decided to see each other when I came back to Fort Worth again.

Friends of ours had encouraged me to move back to Cowtown, and when my divorce was final I decided to do just that. I had lived in Austin since becoming a lawyer, but I had always considered Fort Worth to be home. My parents, my older brother, and many of my close friends lived in Fort Worth, and it was natural for me to return to my roots.

Jacque and I continued to see and get to know each other again, and one thing led to another. On June 11, 1994, we were married at the home of Jacque's son, with a number of our high school classmates in attendance, along with several of her children and several of mine. Something that could have started in the late 1940s and early 1950s finally did start in 1994. I was sixty-one years old, and Jacque was sixty, so our golden years have been experienced together.

I consider myself very fortunate to have had the opportunity to get to know Ben Hogan personally for a few years before his death, and I have come to know him even better doing the research for this book and listening to Jacque tell stories about her Uncle Ben. I also feel honored to be able to convey these stories about the Hogan family to readers. Writing this book has been challenging as well as enjoyable. The Hogan family history could be anyone's, but in many ways it is unique. This was a solid family although not wealthy or famous.

The Hogan family history is one of survival and determination, and this includes Jacque's life. Her family has always been very private, never seeking publicity or notoriety. So much has been written about Ben Hogan, but very little in depth about his personal life. And nothing has been written about the personal lives of other members of the Hogan family.

Many qualified authors have written about Ben Hogan's golf history, and done their job well. This book is not about golf except to the extent that golf was a major part of the men, Royal and Ben Hogan. Jacque is the last surviving descendant in the Chester Hogan family to be born a Hogan. She alone knows much of the true story about this unique family, which was historically committed to a code of silence concerning private family matters. Jacque always adhered to this practice of privacy and was very reluctant to break the silence. Jacque knows the story because she lived it, and she has carefully considered the decision to tell the story as she knows it. There are some statements of opinion here that cannot be backed up with facts, but those opinions were offered honestly, with no intent to offend.

Ultimately, the reader is the final judge. It is my hope that you find much to enjoy as you discover new insights into this unique American family.

ROBERT LINDLEY TOWERY

Coauthors Robert and Jacque Towery.
Jacqueline Hogan Towery family collection
(hereafter JHT family collection).

1

A POINT IN TIME

On February 13, 1922, Chester Hogan boarded the Frisco in Dublin, Texas, and rode the train seventy-five miles northeast to the Texas & Pacific rail station in Fort Worth. In an attempt to satisfy his wife that he would search for a job once again, Chester had agreed to come to the big city to look for work. Yet, all the while, it was actually his sincere hope to bring his family back with him to their home in Dublin. It had been six months since his wife, Clara, had convinced her husband to relocate to Fort Worth and look for better opportunities for their three children. Also, she hoped this would help her husband since Fort Worth was the nearest city with a hospital capable of treating his recent, increasing bouts of melancholy. He originally came with Clara when the entire family made the move in August of 1921, but after a couple of months, in which he could not find work, he returned to his diminishing blacksmith operation in Dublin.

On this day in February 1922, after more unsuccessful job hunting in Fort Worth, Chester returned to the small frame house at 305 Hemphill Street that Clara had rented for the family. Chester pleaded with his wife to return with him to Dublin and their previous familiar routine. Clara didn't like the idea of taking the children out of school before the spring semester was completed, however. They discussed the matter, and then argued loudly enough for the children to hear from another room. At the end of the argument, Chester stormed out and stomped down a small hallway into another room at the back of the house. His twelve-year-old son, Royal, followed him into the room.

As Chester started to rummage through his valise, Royal blurted out, "What are you going to do Daddy?"

Without answering, Chester pulled a .38 caliber revolver from his bag, aimed it at his chest, cocked it, and pulled the trigger. Clara, fifteen-year-old Princess, and nine-year-old Ben ran into the room and saw Royal standing near their wounded father, who was lying on the floor and bleeding. Chester looked up and said, "I wish I hadn't done that."

He was picked up by a Spelman Ambulance and rushed to Protestant Hospital. It was first thought that he would survive, but he did not. He died twelve hours later.

When reporting the suicide the next day, two of the three local Fort Worth papers, the *Press* and the *Record*, reported erroneously that a six-year-old or nine-year-old son witnessed his father's suicide. However, the *Fort Worth Star-Telegram* got it right with its headline: FATHER'S SHOT IS REPLY TO BOY.

The article in the *Star-Telegram* went on to describe how the twelve-year-old Royal had put the query to his father right before he pulled the trigger. The report went on to quote Clara Hogan as saying that her husband had been ill for over a year, and he also had financial worries.

Clara, her daughter, Princess, and her two sons, Royal and Ben, did not discuss the incident with anyone for many, many years.

LEFT TO RIGHT: Clara and Chester (rear), Ben, Princess, and Royal Hogan (front), about 1919.
JHT family collection.

But as a result of the two error-filled newspaper reports that referred to a nine-year old child being in the room, it was long assumed by many people that Ben was the child who witnessed his father's suicide. This led to mistaken articles, and then these articles were used as references in biographies about Ben Hogan, some going so far as saying Ben's steely disposition and hardened reserve on

Alex Hogan and his son Chester, with two blacksmiths in
front of the Hogan General Repair and Horse Shoeing Shop.
JHT family collection.

the golf course resulted from the fact that he had witnessed his father shoot himself. Since young Ben was in the house when the tragedy occurred, it would seem natural that an event such as this would mark a child in some way. However, his niece Jacqueline ("Jacque") Hogan Towery, who was very close to her uncle, totally disagrees that the suicide molded his essence.

JACQUE: *Mama Hogan (Clara) had a disciplined philosophy and perfectionist attitude, and it was those characteristics that had the most effect on Uncle Ben and my dad, Royal, as well. She taught them to persevere while they were growing up, especially during the Depression. Mama Hogan taught Uncle Ben and my daddy a strong work ethic that strengthened their resolve and helped make them the successful men they eventually became.*

Why hadn't Ben Hogan set the record straight?

JACQUE: *Late in his life, Uncle Ben told me once, "I had been misquoted my whole career and there were also so many falsities from third person narratives, that I tired of trying to set the record straight. I decided not to deal with the misinformation, so I just let it all go." You see, the Hogan family was very private—we just never talked about things like this. So, the people who wrote those books and reported that Uncle Ben saw his father kill himself were never informed of the* mistake. *To this day there are a lot of people who don't know the real story, because nobody in the family ever talked about it. I was almost in college before I knew the story. I was told one time, and that was it. It was never discussed again.*

During the waning years of Royal Hogan's life, when he was in his eighties, his grandson, Dr. David Corley, and Corley's wife Dayna would pick up "Pops," as they affectionately called Jacque's father, and take him to dinner, usually once or twice a week. They would always offer to take him to various new restaurants they thought he would enjoy, but Pops never wanted to try anything out of his element. He preferred to go to one of his staples, like Joe T. Garcia's for Mexican food, Lone Star Oyster Bar for the fried shrimp, or his favorite late in his life, Olive Garden. Royal loved to eat their salad with breadsticks.

Dayna related, "At dinner one night at Olive Garden, Pops opened up to us about his father. According to Pops, he thought the fact his father took his own life was because his mother wouldn't go back to Dublin. And then, Pops said the books reported their dad shot himself in front of Ben, but he added, 'That's not true. He shot himself in front of me.' He told me that story one time, but I remember it succinctly."

David added, "When he did tell us, it was a long, drawn-out story. It was not just volunteered; it was about thirty minutes of conversation. When he finished, he was wiping tears from his eyes. I never saw more emotion in Pops than he showed that night."

Jacque always pondered what would have happened if her grandfather hadn't taken his life when he did.

JACQUE: *One has to consider what might've been different if that moment in my family's past had never happened. Would my father have become a successful businessman? Would he have quit school when he did? Would he or Uncle Ben have attended college? And, most importantly, would Daddy or Uncle Ben have ever picked up the game of golf? I wonder.*

2

PANTHER CITY TO COWTOWN TO BOOMTOWN

One can't discuss the Hogan family, their friends, supporters, customers, or their importance to Fort Worth without looking at the history and development of the city itself. It appears that three years in particular became important watermarks in the birth of Fort Worth as a major city: 1876, 1902, and 1917.

After the Civil War, many future prominent citizens relocated their families from other states in the South to Fort Worth. Among these were Major K. M. Van Zandt, Captain E. M. Daggett, Thomas J. Jennings, John Peter Smith, and H. G. Hendricks. This group of five men knew the importance of having rail service and what it could bring to their small town. In the early 1870s, the Texas & Pacific Railroad (known as the "T&P") was building a rail line from Dallas to Fort Worth, but unfortunately a company underwriting the construction went bankrupt in 1872. With that the line stopped just west of Dallas—still more than twenty miles from Fort Worth. At this point, a mass exodus brought Fort Worth down from a population close to five thousand to less than one thousand souls. One local lawyer wrote to the *Dallas Morning News* and said that the town was so deserted he saw a panther sleeping at a downtown intersection. After this report, the Dallas newspaper began to refer to the sleepy town to its west as "Pantherville." The term

Panther City sprang from that article and became synonymous with Fort Worth for many years to follow.

Van Zandt and the others were undaunted, however. They knew the value of the railroad and were determined to bring it to their town. These men were five of the most resourceful civic leaders in Fort Worth's early history.

Khleber Miller (K. M.) Van Zandt, who rose to be a major in the Confederacy, had been a lawyer in Marshall, Texas, prior to the Civil War. After the conflict ended, in 1866, he moved to Fort Worth and became an attorney, a merchant, and a reluctant politician, representing the city in the state legislature for several years. Van Zandt was the president of the Fort Worth National Bank for over fifty years, and for his many valuable contributions to the city and its people, he became known as "Mr. Fort Worth."

After the Civil War Captain Ephraim (E. M.) Daggett also migrated to Fort Worth, where he built the first hotel in the city. He purchased quite a bit of land in the area, and together with Van Zandt, Jennings, Smith, and Hendricks donated 320 acres of land south of Fort Worth for the construction of a railroad station. The city later named elementary and junior high schools in Daggett's honor.

Thomas J. Jennings was one of the first true statesmen in the city of Fort Worth. He was a major landowner and a very distinguished lawyer, and served the state of Texas as its attorney general for several years. In his memory, the city named one of its major thoroughfares, Jennings Avenue, as well as Jennings Junior High School, after him.

After attending three colleges, Kentuckian John Peter Smith arrived in Fort Worth in 1853. He was a surveyor, lawyer, real estate magnate, and philanthropist who became known as "The Father of Fort Worth" (not to be confused with Van Zandt's moniker, "Mr. Fort Worth"). Smith was elected mayor in 1882 and served six terms. During his tenure, he was a key figure in establishing and developing the city's first water department and in developing the stockyards. Mayor Smith also started the independent public school system, where he taught for several years, and served as a school board trustee. He was a cofounder of the Fort Worth National Bank and was the president of the very successful Fort Worth Gas Light and Coal Company. During his lifetime, John Peter Smith became the largest landowner in the area, and donated much of his land to the city for utilities, churches, parks, and a hospital that still bears his name today.

Judge H. G. Hendricks was born in Missouri in 1819 and was a direct descendant of the Mayflower's Miles Standish. Hendricks moved to Texas in 1845 to study law un-

Fort Worth in the 1880s.
Courtesy *Fort Worth Star-Telegram* Collection, Special Collections, the University of Texas at Arlington Library, Arlington, Texas (hereafter FWST/UTA).

der Judge G. A. Evarts in Bonham, Texas. In 1846, Hendricks became an attorney and relocated to Fort Worth to practice law. He was later appointed a district judge and emerged as one of the most respected and revered men in the city. In his honor, Fort Worth named a roadway Hendricks Street.

Under the leadership of Van Zandt and these four men, the community organized the Tarrant County Construction Company. The capital stock was subscribed in money, labor, and supplies, and the citizens of Fort Worth pitched in and helped to complete the construction of the Dallas-Fort Worth railroad, laying the final tracks into Fort Worth proper. On July 19, 1876, people from all over West Texas flooded to the city center to see a railroad engine, the first ever to arrive in Fort Worth, pull into the Texas & Pacific depot, a small wooden structure on South Main just west of what is now Lancaster Avenue.

Once this feat was accomplished, Fort Worth never faced mass exodus again. By 1900, the city had grown to a population of twenty-five thousand. The city became the center for the shipping of West Texas beef to the rest of the nation. From 1876 to 1900, over four million head of cattle were transported by train from Fort Worth—first from the T&P station, and then, beginning in 1889, from the Union Stockyards the city had built under the direction of Mayor John Pe-

ter Smith—to meatpacking facilities in such cities as Kansas City, St. Louis, Chicago, and other destinations around the nation. As Fort Worth grew, so did its institutions—banks, newspapers, and local retailers, all led by its earliest movers and shakers. In 1902, the city leaders succeeded in attracting Swift and Company, Armour and Company, and McNeill & Libby, and each built meatpacking plants at the Stockyards in north Fort Worth. It was during this period that the city began to be known as "Cowtown" and really started to prosper.

New developers saw opportunity in the growing city. One of the key people in this subsequent development was William Bryce, a transplanted Scotsman, who dearly loved the city. Bryce, mayor of Fort Worth from 1927 to 1933, was a bricklayer by trade, and before the turn of the century he joined with two Denver real estate entrepreneurs, Alfred W. and H. B. Chamberlain, to develop a new suburb west of downtown which became known as Arlington Heights. Bryce's house, Fairview, was constructed in 1893, and was one of the rare examples of Château-style homes in Texas. It featured Richardsonian arches and gabled dormers and was designed by the prominent architectural firm of Messer, Sanguinet, and Messer, who were responsible for many of the famous landmark turn-of-the-century buildings and homes in

Fort Worth in the 1930s.
Courtesy FWST/UTA.

Fort Worth. Fairview, which still stands today at 4900 Bryce Avenue, was one of the first homes built in the Heights. Bryce was among those responsible for developing the Fort Worth Club in 1903 as part of the development of Arlington Heights, constructing a main building for entertaining, several tennis courts, and the city's first nine-hole golf course. By 1911, the club members had splintered over their growth and direction into the future. The club was closed, and this division begat the River Crest Country Club and Fort Worth's first eighteen-hole golf course, built in 1912. For those who were not allowed to join River Crest, like H. H. Cobb of the O. K. Cattle Company, another group built the Glen Garden Golf and Country Club a few miles southeast of Fort Worth on land donated by Cobb. Those two eighteen-hole golf courses survive today—both built in 1912, which just happened to be the same year Sam Snead and Fort Worth legends Ben Hogan and Byron Nelson were born.

During the first two decades of the twentieth century, Cowtown was growing into a city, yet it was still in the shadow of its much larger neighbor, Dallas. But little Cowtown was about to explode. In 1917, oil was discovered in Ranger, ninety miles west of Fort Worth, and subsequently in nearby Breckenridge, Desdemona, and Burkburnett. These sites came through with gushers and literally turned Cowtown into a boomtown. Speculators, operators, geologists, oil companies, mavericks, and wildcatters flooded into the city and set up business. This wave of activity started in the Westbrook Hotel. It was reported that a speculator could purchase a lease entering one side of the lobby and sell it on the way out the other side. The oil booms combined with the railroads, cattle shipping, and meatpacking plants to change the landscape of Fort Worth forever, bringing national attention to a booming city where panthers used to sleep.

3

THE EARLY YEARS

Chester Hogan was twenty-three and Clara Williams Hogan was only eighteen when they started having children. Their first child was born in Dublin, Texas, on April 25, 1907. She was a pretty little girl they named Chester Princess Hogan.

JACQUE: *I never heard an explanation of why my aunt was named Chester, but I suspect that my grandfather wanted a boy, so he insisted that the child be named after him. Thankfully, she was also given the name Princess, by which she would be known. Princess always leaned toward the more domestic interests when she was a youngster, such as cooking, housework, and gardening. She loved music and performed in several musicals while in school. I was told that she also did some acting in local productions. Princess was the only member of the family to attend college. While attending college, she met H. Howard Ditto, who was from a well-to-do Arlington family. In the 1920's era, his parents were early prominent citizens of the town east of Fort Worth, and they owned and ran the very successful Arlington Seed Company. Doc, as he was called, became a doctor and he married Aunt Princess. She was destined to become an excellent homemaker and a wonderful wife.*

A second Hogan child, Royal Dean (Jacque's father) was born February 16, 1909. While growing up in Dublin, Royal developed his natural athletic abilities. Among other activities, he formed a baseball team.

Royal Hogan (center, front row) with his
Dublin Elementary School classmates, around 1919.
JHT family collection.

JACQUE: *In those days, there were no organized leagues or sponsored teams, but Daddy scraped up enough players to form a team, and there were always enough other boys around to make up a team to play against.*

Royal was the star pitcher, and many folks thought he would end up playing professional baseball. There is no question that Royal was a multi-talented man.

JACQUE: *Daddy also played the violin and the clarinet, and he was actually good. One of the first times I heard him playing the violin, I mistakenly asked him, "Where did you learn to play the fiddle?" He replied, "This is not a fiddle, it's a violin." Unfortunately, I never found out how he learned to play musical instruments.*

In his later years, at dinner with his grandson David Corley and David's wife Dayna, Royal would wax poetic about those early days in Dublin.

Dayna Corley recalled, "Pops (Royal) talked about being in Dublin often. He would relate stories about his dad as a blacksmith. He talked about his grandfather, who he really liked, and he loved to talk about playing baseball and going to school in Dublin."

JACQUE: *However, once the family moved to Fort Worth, my daddy never went back to Dublin, He never even showed any interest in going back.*

Chester Hogan holds baby Ben, with Royal and Princess
JHT family collection.

Then, on August 13, 1912, Chester and Clara's third and last child, another son, was delivered by Dr. J. J. Mulloy at a hospital in Stephenville, a town near Dublin. Most children in those days were born at home, so perhaps Clara was having some difficulty with her pregnancy. After discussing a possible name for the youngster, they named him William Ben Hogan after his two grandfathers. Little Ben growing up in Dublin was just a kid growing up in a small Texas town who occasionally enjoyed riding horseback with his dad. It was clear that Ben Hogan loved his father very much.

Chester Hogan on horseback with baby Ben.
JHT family collection.

THE MOVE TO FORT WORTH

ROBERT: *Chester became noticeably ill in early 1921. He often thought about death and at times was unable to work. He was drinking more than ever, and his moods varied from one extreme to the other. His health worsened as the blacksmith trade became less and less needed in the area. The nearest hospital that could treat Chester's condition was a sanatorium in Fort Worth. Clara Hogan knew that the doctors in Dublin could not diagnose his problem, much less treat it. In those days, mental depression was called melancholia or a nervous disorder or a "mal-ady of the spirit." There were not many hospitals in Texas where one could seek help. Yet Clara had an uncommon "common sense" and the instinct to know when something needed to be done. She made the critical decision to move the family from Dublin to the lively boomtown of Fort Worth.*

Jacque's daughter-in-law, Dayna Corley said, "Pops told us he did not want to move away from Dublin when he was a kid. I think it broke the boys' hearts, probably Princess's too, when his mom moved them to Fort Worth."

Jacque believes that it was probably the best thing that could have happened to them. "But it must have been tough," Jacque's son David maintained. "They were only nine, twelve, and fifteen years old, and they were used to the country and suddenly, they moved to the big city of Fort Worth."

In Fort Worth, Clara rented a small frame house on Hemphill Street just south of downtown, and Chester began outpatient treatment at the nearby hospital. But when he could not find work as a mechanic, he abruptly returned to Dublin and reopened his blacksmith shop.

An accomplished seamstress, Clara had no trouble finding work in Fort Worth at women's dress shops, mainly at Cheney's and Wally Williams. Cheney's was one of the first ladies' exceptional apparel stores in downtown Fort Worth—hats, dresses, everything for women—a very high-end establishment. Wally Williams was in the same mode as Cheney's, carrying only ladies' fine clothes. Meacham's was also high-end, but it and the more moderate Striplings, R. E. Cox, and The Fair were department stores. They had women's departments, but they also carried men's and children's clothing, domestic goods, and many other products as well.

JACQUE: *Mama Hogan taught me to sew when I was twelve years old, and I learned in a hurry not to cross her. She was a real taskmaster and would say, "Do it right or don't do it at all." She expected sewing to be done perfectly, which meant her way. When I was young, she could be as sweet as pie, but she didn't show that very often. And when she was determined, look out! It made a difference to her about sewing the absolute best it could be done, for she was a perfectionist. This disciplined attitude was a quality she bestowed on her children and a philosophy she applied to everything. When she was teaching me, if a seam on a sleeve had the tiniest flaw, I mean the smallest pucker, I would have to take it all apart and start over until I got it right. She was tough, but because of her quest for perfection, I became an accomplished seamstress, sewing all my clothes from age twelve on. I made everything I wore, including pants, skirts, jackets, and evening wear.*

She taught me well, and thank goodness for that.

It is not clear what Chester's actual clinical diagnosis was. He was an outpatient for only a brief period in 1921 before he returned to Dublin. The hospital has since burned down, and all records were destroyed. However, hindsight tells us that his ailment was probably bipolar disorder, with its alternating manic and depressive episodes—a condition known to be complicated by alcohol consumption. In any event, as 1921 turned into 1922, Chester had enough of his wits about him to know that he missed his family.

With the hope of bringing his family back to Dublin, Chester returned to Fort Worth on February 13, 1922, a day that would end in a horrible tragedy.

ROBERT: *Chester's body was taken back to Dublin, where he was buried in the Old Dublin Cemetery, close to his mother Cynthia, who died in 1907. His father, William Alexander Hogan, died in 1936 and is buried in the family plot, along with Clara's parents, Benjamin Hicks and Lelia Prentiss Williams, and several of Clara's siblings.*

Shortly after Chester's death and burial, Clara packed everything and moved the children from the Hemphill Street house to an apartment on Taylor Street. This was closer to her job at Cheney's and within walking

The monument for Chester Hogan at the Old Dublin Cemetery, now called the Old Dublin Memorial Park. JHT family collection.

distance from two other stores at which she could get work. Soon thereafter, she heard about a house for rent at 1316 East Allen Avenue, which would be closer to the children's school. Shortly after moving to East Allen, she enrolled Princess, Royal, and Ben in Sunday school at the Evans Avenue Baptist Church, just a few blocks away. At this church, Royal would meet his future bride, Margaret Duncan, who lived about nine blocks from the Hogan's home.

JACQUE: *No matter how hard Mama Hogan worked, there was never enough income to raise three children, and she finally and reluctantly allowed my father to quit school in the sixth grade and go to work to help the family. I don't think he cared whether Mama Hogan wished he would continue with school or not. He quit to help her raise the family, and he never went back. Princess also helped out when she could by babysitting neighborhood children after school, and later on she worked part time at a local drugstore. At first, my father sold newspapers downtown on Seventh Street, right outside the* Fort Worth Star-Telegram *offices, where he had to fight for the best spot. He later convinced his mother that it would be all right for Ben to come down after school and help him sell his papers. Ben was in the fourth grade at Carroll Peak Elementary School and wanted to help. Daddy took young Uncle Ben to the T & P Railroad station, gave him some papers, and returned to his Seventh Street location. When he had sold all of his papers, Daddy would go back to the station where he would try to help Ben sell the remainder of his. Very often they would then go to a hamburger stand near the courthouse for a burger, fries, and a soda pop for the grand total of five cents. During this time, they discovered*

Present day photo of one of the houses
that the Hogan brothers grew up in,
at 1316 East Allen Avenue in Fort Worth.
JHT family collection.

another means of making some money—by carrying luggage for train passengers. They had to do this on the sly, of course, knowing this was not appreciated by the official porters. This was "Red Cap" territory, and the tips were supposed to go to the railroad porters. The boys knew they would get in trouble if they ever got caught. I remember my daddy telling me about a day when a Red Cap saw them and gave chase, and he and Ben had to drop the bags they were carrying and run for their lives. That was the end of that.

A friend at school told Ben that he could make more money at a golf course carrying golf bags for the players. Once you were recognized as a first-rate caddy, Ben learned, you were allowed to carry double—that is, carry for two golfers. This meant double pay and double tips. So, the next summer, Ben trekked the six miles out to the Glen Garden Golf and Country Club to become a caddy. Ben was unaware of what he was stepping into, however, and did not find an open door. Caddies were in abundance, and they did not look favorably upon newcomers digging into their treasure. New kids were discouraged in every way possible. A "wannabe" caddy had to run the gauntlet—two lines of established caddies with belts in their hands—and the new prospect was lashed by each boy as he ran between the two lines. A further test awaited Ben when the big kids stuffed him into a barrel made of curved wooden staves and rolled it down a hill behind the clubhouse. It was a forty-yard roll with a twenty-foot drop. At the bottom of the hill the barrel broke apart, and young Ben picked himself up, not knowing if he had any broken bones.

JACQUE: *Uncle Ben was a scrapper. He told me they still made him fight one of the larger boys as a final test to become a caddy, and he got the better of this fellow because he knew how to fight.*

Sooner or later the boys who wanted it badly enough made the grade to become a caddy, and Ben made it. He began to carry bags for golfers—and more importantly began the

A young Royal Hogan in Fort Worth (probably early 1920s). JHT family collection.

walk that would ultimately lead to his domination of the game itself. Many caddies also played golf, and it wasn't long until Ben got the bug. The only club he could find was a left-handed mashie (an iron), and he would hit golf balls with it each weekend morning before the golfers arrived. The caddies had a

Ben, Princess, and Royal Hogan.
JHT family collection.

continuing contest wherein each boy would hit the ball as far as he could, and the loser had to go fetch all the balls. Ben Hogan was never last. One day each month the caddies were allowed to play the course, and it wasn't long before Ben knew that this was what he wanted to do for the rest of his life.

JACQUE: *Unfortunately, though he had found his calling, it was around this time that my Uncle Ben also started smoking cigarettes. It was a habit he continued into his eighties—usually about two packs a day.*

At Glen Garden, the caddies got in a lot of practice before the members showed up, and as Ben's skills grew in the sport, he tried to get his older brother to come out and give it a try.

JACQUE: *Daddy was convinced that Uncle Ben was wasting his time, and my father would have none of that. He told Ben that hitting a little white ball around a field was the stupidest thing he'd ever heard of, but his brother persisted. Finally, to get Ben to shut up and leave him alone, he said he would go. And after a few times of walking to Glen Garden with Uncle Ben and caddying for the members, my father began to show an interest in the game. Daddy turned out to be a natural talent. He told me he was hooked after the first time he swung a golf club. The rest is Hogan family history. It's ironic that these two kids from Dublin, who had never seen a golf course until they caddied at Glen Garden, would accomplish all that they did.*

Young Ben had to work hard at golf. This is where his very strict practice routine was first developed. He learned that he could get extra roll and thus move the ball farther if he hooked the ball. This seemed to be natural for Ben, and it enabled him to win most of the driving contests with the other caddies. It would become a huge problem for him, however, once he started pursuing a career as a professional golfer.

It was during this early period that Royal convinced Ben to switch to right-handed clubs. Ben was a natural right-hander, but the only club he owned was a left-handed iron with a wooden shaft. Royal explained to Ben that good used left-handed clubs would be extremely difficult to find.

JACQUE: *I don't know when Uncle Ben got a complete set of clubs, but I'm certain that it was probably a mixed set of different brands. One day, and how, I don't know, Mama Hogan saved forty dollars to purchase Uncle Ben a true set of clubs, and I'm sure that Daddy and Aunt Princess pitched in. Golf was the perfect game for Uncle Ben's fondness for solitude and his ability to concentrate. He was able to work alone, without teammates, and to accept all the credit or blame for the results. Golf provided competition, and if nothing else, Uncle Ben was very competitive, either by nature or through the concentrated determination he learned from his mother. Uncle Ben told me once that golf gave him, at a young age, a feeling of being worthwhile.*

Golf also gave Royal and Ben the opportunity to meet and become friends with department store magnate Marvin Leonard and oilmen like W. A. Moncrief, his son, Tex, Earl Baldridge, Neville Penrose, and others. They would all have a major impact on the Hogan brothers' development as men and as players in the game of golf, business, and life.

4

TWO BROTHERS COME OF AGE

As they were pursuing business and golf, the two brothers also became interested in their social lives. During their early teen years, Clara, or "Mama Hogan," had enrolled Royal, Ben, and their older sister, Princess, in Sunday school class at Evans Avenue Baptist Church. It was there that Royal met Margaret Duncan, who grew up on Jessamine Street not far from the church and just down the block from the Hogans' home. The two grew close, and eventually they fell for each other. On December 16, 1925, when Royal and Margaret were both sixteen years old, they eloped.

JACQUE: *Daddy told her parents he was taking my mother to church, but instead, they ran off and got married.*

Royal and Margaret settled in at a house on East Pulaski Street, a few blocks north-west of Mama Hogan's and the Duncans' homes. Margaret's parents, Harry M. Duncan and Myrtle "BB" Chrisman, had married in Fort Worth soon after the turn of the twentieth century.

JACQUE: *My grandmother, BB, as I called her, was a magnificent cook—she could bake, roast, or fry anything. I remember the hot water cornbread, fried chicken and cream gravy, black-eyed peas, and corn she used to make when I was young. They lived about a block off Evans Avenue, and their backyard had a cow, horses, goats, chickens, pigs, and ducks, along with an extensive vegetable garden. For a living, they made sandwiches in the back part of their house, and Harry, my grandfather, or "PawPaw" as I called him, would deliver the various sandwiches to drugstores, lunch counters, and different*

ABOVE Myrtle Duncan in front of the Duncans' home at 725 Jefferson in Fort Worth. JHT family collection.

LEFT Royal and Margaret Hogan pose in front of the home of her parents, Harry and Myrtle Duncan, in the 1930s. JHT family collection.

places. Those sandwiches were very, very good and they provided a living for them for many years. When Interstate 35 was being constructed, their house was condemned to make way for the freeway, and they moved to Forest Park Boulevard.

B. B.'s brother, Edd Chrisman, was one of Jacque's favorite grown-ups when she was young. Uncle Edd, as everyone called him, would visit from time to time when the circus that employed him as its resident strong man took an annual hiatus.

JACQUE: *In the circus, Uncle Edd was famous as the "strongest man in the world." He was a lot of fun. Every time he visited he would bring me a Kewpie doll.*

George Wilkes was Edd Chrisman's nephew and spent time with him when he was a youngster, recalling, "Uncle Edd was the only boy in the family. Besides working as a strongman, he also worked the midway, sometimes as a barker but mostly running various booths like the ring-toss or rifle gallery. His pockets were always full of dimes from patrons attempting to win Kewpie dolls."

JACQUE: *That was when a dime was a dime.*

After he had stopped caddying at Glen Garden, Royal decided to move on, finding work delivering office supplies on his bicycle for Bert Pollard & Company. He didn't make much more money as Pollard's delivery boy than he had double-bagging twice a day as a

Harry Duncan holds a family duck in front of their home in Fort Worth. JHT family collection.

Edd Chrisman, "the strongest man in the world," demonstrates his strength supporting a car full of GIs on his stomach. JHT family collection.

caddy, but Royal knew he wanted to become a businessman and decided this would provide him the learning opportunity that would help him realize his own goals someday.

He worked for several years for Bert Pollard before landing a position with the L. A. Barnes Company. Pollard and Barnes were the two most successful office supply companies in Fort Worth during the boom years. The young Royal Hogan impressed both employers with his work ethic and desire to advance. L. A. Barnes, in particular, decided to take Royal under his wing and taught him everything about the business. Royal was eager to learn and even attended night school to study bookkeeping and accounting. He had a quick grasp of numbers, like his maternal grandfather Ben Williams, but even so, his skills were surprising for a young man with only a sixth-grade education.

JACQUE: *My daddy told me that he always knew he wanted to run his own successful business. He was a self-made man. He could figure math faster than you could do it on the calculator—add, subtract, divide—he was amazing. And his English was impeccable. He could do all kinds of math and was an excellent speller. I don't know how he learned it, but he did.*

His first venture into his own office supply business was eventful. In 1932, Royal Hogan and a partner who was to help manage the sales opened the Fort Worth Office Supply Company in a very small space on Throckmorton Street, just off the alley behind the public library. After being in business for several months, the partner approached Royal for more control of the business, which Royal declined. He knew from his experiences with sole proprietorships like Pollard and Barnes that establishing a business where he could maintain complete control was the only way to go. So Royal made the decision to buy out his partner, deciding it was best for him to go it alone. And he did so in a big way.

In 1935, Royal borrowed a small amount of money and moved his business to a larger location at 911 Houston Street. In the beginning there were some lean times, as the Depression wouldn't really end until World War II started several years later. However, Fort Worth was in the midst of an oil boom, and the businesses that utilized Fort Worth Office Supply products were already flourishing. It was because of the ongoing loyalty of those oil companies and other growing businesses

Royal Hogan and his dog. Behind them is the bike Royal used to deliver office supplies for the L. A. Barnes Co. JHT family collection.

that Royal was able to pay off his initial loan in six months. Hogan's Fort Worth Office Supply Company remained debt free for the next fifty years.

JACQUE: *As far as I know, Daddy only borrowed money twice in his life: once was to open his business downtown, and the other time, years later, to build his house on Alton Road. He paid both of those loans back in six months. I always felt this had everything to do with his mistrust of banks that had crashed during the Depression.*

After several years at 911 Houston, Royal moved his Fort Worth Office Supply to 1007 Main Street, where he could have a larger showroom. Royal ran a tight ship from the beginning. In the early days during the Depression, a customer might come in for one pencil, or one page of carbon paper, and maybe ten sheets of typing paper—and that might have been a good sale. But Royal saw that future growth in his business would not come from selling paper products, pencils, and erasers, so he added office furniture, desks, file cabinets, office lamps, and other durable goods to his inventory. This enabled Royal to hire a floor staff and a sales staff, bookkeepers, and eventually even family members to work for him, always under his watchful eye and dictatorial control.

A few doors away from Royal's Fort Worth Office Supply were offices for the very successful Moncrief Oil Company that was started by W. A. Moncrief in 1929. Moncrief was one of the greatest wildcatters in Texas history. He was born in Sulphur Springs, Texas, in 1895, but his family had moved to Oklahoma before he attended high school. Learning how to type and take shorthand as a teenager enabled W. A. to raise enough money as a court reporter in Eufala, Oklahoma, that he could pay for his own tuition to attend the University of Oklahoma. It was at OU that his fraternity brothers gave him his lifelong nickname, "Monty."

World War I interrupted college, and Monty voluntarily enlisted in the US Cavalry, where he was sent to officer training camp in Little Rock, Arkansas, to be trained in machine guns. In Little Rock, he met Mary Elizabeth Bright. He married her in May of 1918. Monty was soon transferred to France but saw no combat, as the Armistice was signed before he ever saw any action.

After the war, he and Mary Elizabeth returned to Oklahoma, where he joined the Marland Oil Company in their accounting department. After a few short years, he had risen to be the vice president of the company's land department, located in Fort Worth. By 1929, he was ready to strike off on his own, gambling that, as an independent oilman, he could strike it rich. He teamed up with John Ferrell during the Depression, and became a very wealthy man when they were able to acquire mineral rights on some land in East Texas. They drilled the F. K. Lathrop #1, and it was a gusher. Their lease was on the northernmost extension of the East Texas field, at that time one of the largest deposits of oil ever discovered. Monty's good fortunes continued for his entire lifetime, with discoveries spanning many states, and very seldom did his team drill a duster.

Monty and his partner and oldest son, Tex, became lifelong friends of Royal Hogan.

Monty, a very good golfer and sports enthusiast, introduced Royal to other oilmen and various businessmen, many of whom became customers of Fort Worth Office Supply. This proved fruitful not only for Royal's business, but also for his personal wealth through the independent investments he made with various friends of commerce over the years.

Tex Moncrief reflected, "My dad would be playing golf with a couple of other oil men, and they would invite Royal to play with them. Royal would listen in on the conversations about upcoming investment opportunities in the oilfields, and he would shuttle over and say, 'Can I get a little bit of that?' Royal never invested more than one percent, but you have to realize on a million dollar deal, that would have been an investment of $10,000, which was a good sum of money in the forties and fifties. Most of the wells we drilled in those days were successful, so Royal had a pretty good return on his 'little bit of that'!"

Through Royal's association and friendship with prominent, wealthy, successful men, mostly at lunch or on the golf course, the number of successful companies on Fort Worth Office Supply's customer list grew almost exponentially those early years.

In 1935, ten years after their sudden marriage, Royal Hogan, his wife Margaret, and their three-year-old daughter Jacqueline moved from the house on East Pulaski to a two-bedroom home at 3420 Childress Street in southeast Fort Worth.

There was more than one reason to move to Childress Street. The house was only two short blocks from Oak Lawn Elementary, where Jacqueline would start school in a couple of years—and more important for Royal, their new home was only a few blocks from Glen Garden, the country club where Royal had caddied over a decade before. During the mid-1930s, Royal's new office supply business was growing, and its success allowed him to join Glen Garden. Royal had grown from caddy to club member, from dropout to success in a short twelve years, which included some of the worst times of the horrible Depression that had such a sour grip on the nation.

The home life on Childress was a simple one for Royal, Margaret, and little Jacqueline. Two bedrooms, one of which was very large, one bath, a kitchen, a breakfast room, living room, and a porch made up the entirety of their home, with good-sized front and back yards and an empty lot next to the house. From Jacqueline's earliest memories, her family had a housekeeper at the Childress house to look after the daily chores. Frances Jones, in her midthirties, was a gregarious lady who had a house down the street and took care of young Jacqueline. She cooked

ABOVE Royal Hogan and his young daughter
Jacqueline in a vintage little red wagon.
JHT family collection.

LEFT Frances Jones, the Hogans'
housekeeper and nanny for Jacqueline.
JHT family collection.

no doubt that Valerie had put it there, and from then on she guarded against Valerie being alone in a room with baby Sarah. This was a weird twist on Valerie's reputation as a very shy girl who never uttered an ill word about anyone.

Ben used to relate that he met Valerie while attending Jennings Junior High School, although Valerie always said they met during their first year at Central High.

JACQUE: *I tend to believe what Mama Hogan always said—that they met in Sunday school at the Evans Avenue Baptist Church very near their homes. Uncle Ben was attracted to Valerie Fox because she was very pretty. Uncle Ben valued loyalty very highly, and he needed someone who loved him, was loyal to him, trusted him, and believed in him. Valerie had these qualities. Valerie, on the other hand, needed someone with good character who could give her strength, someone who had ambition and aspired to be someone special.*

The Fox family had moved to Cleburne in 1930, so when Ben landed his club pro job two years later, he began to court Valerie. They were married at her parents' house in April of 1935. Mama Hogan had expressed reservations about Valerie Fox, but she never said anything to Ben. She did not attend her son's wedding, as she was conveniently visiting her daughter Princess and son-in-law Doc, who was finishing his residency in Los Angeles, California.

Those early years were lean economically as Ben suffered with his game on and off the tour, and even with all of the loving support from Valerie, the two would not have survived if it hadn't been for the generosity of a great man Ben met while caddying at Glen Garden when he was fifteen. That man was Marvin Leonard.

5

MR. MARVIN

After WWI, with the continuing discoveries of oil in West Texas and Oklahoma, Fort Worth became a center for the various petroleum industries that were exploring and drilling for "black gold." Dallas still remained the center for banking and finance; Fort Worth's growth was fueled by cattle and oil, along with meatpacking, wheat and cotton, railroad industries, and retail businesses. The population exploded as more and more people relocated from rural communities to the big city to pursue the American dream. Fort Worth had grown from 25,000 people in 1900 to 106,000 in a short seventeen years. During the following period, from 1917 to 1929, many Texans from extremely austere backgrounds became wealthy, self-made men. One of the most inspirational of these was businessman, innovator, developer, and civic leader Marvin Leonard.

Marvin Leonard was born February 10, 1895, on his family's one hundred acre farm near Linden, the county seat of Cass County. The acreage was tucked away in East Texas, not very far from the Louisiana border. His parents, Obadiah and Emma Clementine Leonard, not only farmed the land but also ran a small general store in Linden. The second youngest in a family of nine, Marvin was a frail and sickly child who suffered two serious bouts of pneumonia. His parents, however, made sure that he missed as little schooling as possible, and as he grew into a teenager, Marvin overcame his childhood infirmities as he helped the family out around the farm. He plowed the fields along with two of his brothers, Tom and Obie, and they raised cotton, peanuts, fruit, and vegetables. The boys were also responsible for feeding and tending to the cattle, mules, and chickens.

About a month before he was to graduate, Marvin thought it was best to save the family the expense of buying him a graduation suit, so he quit high school. He got a job for fifty cents a day, driving a buggy full of salesmen around a three-county area as they displayed and sold their goods to various merchants and shops. Along the road, listening to these salesmen discuss the various techniques of the merchants they served, Marvin received his first introduction to the world of business.

When WWI came about, Marvin tried to enlist in the army, but poor vision in one eye and flat feet kept him out of the service. His older brother Tom was living in Dallas, and Marvin decided to join him there to find a better-paying job, in a position he hoped would provide him with greater business acumen. Fortuitously, L. H. Gardiner, who ran a salvage and grocery store business, hired Marvin as an assistant with a starting salary of $27.50 a week. The two would meet at the railroad yards every morning at 4:00 a.m.,

when they would share a shot of whiskey before offering to purchase the unclaimed or damaged freight lying around. They would eventually sell those items later, as discounted products in Gardiner's store. This experience taught Marvin about evaluating merchandise, advertising to attract customers, and purchasing bulk inventories in order to sell larger quantities at lower margins—all practices that boosted Gardiner's profits.

When WWI ended, Marvin decided it was the right time to start his own business, but he didn't want to go into competition with his mentor and employer, Mr. Gardiner, so he moved to Fort Worth. The resourceful Marvin found a grocer who was going out of business and offered to buy his stock. He then sold the products at a discounted rate and turned his meager investment into nearly enough money to open his own store. He fell just short of that, so his father, his brother Tom, and his sister Enola supplied Marvin with some additional funding to make it possible. Marvin rented a twenty-five-foot storefront at 100 North Houston Street, near the Tarrant County Courthouse. He convinced Tom to join him in running the business and their store, Leonard's, opened on December 14, 1918.

From the store's inception, Marvin knew he couldn't and shouldn't compete with the upscale Fort Worth stores offering high-end

Obie and Marvin Leonard soon after
Leonard Brothers opened.
Courtesy of Marty Leonard.

business, Marvin would rush to buy up their inventory. He then sold it at a price no other store could match. Leonard's was a big success from the start, earning a profit from day one.

In 1919, Tom, wanting to go into business on his own, left Leonard's to open a grocery store at the south end of Houston Street. Marvin asked his younger brother, Obie, who was working as a mechanic in Dallas, if he would like to move to Fort Worth and "partner up" in the expansion of his store. Marvin and Obie founded Leonard Brothers in 1919, and the two siblings, who complemented each other extremely well, began to expand the business. Eventually, their store would cover seven city blocks.

Marty Leonard, Marvin's second oldest daughter, who grew up to become one of the best women amateur golfers in the state of Texas, knew well the working relationship between her father and uncle.

"My dad or my uncle would come up with ideas, then follow through on them to increase their business," Marty explained. "Dad was sort of the merchandiser and planner. My uncle, Obie, was the operational guy, as he had the technical know-how for getting a project completed. My dad didn't have anything to do with that. As partners in Leonard Brothers they were a wonderful complement to one another."

merchandise, so he catered to the less-affluent, expanding population by offering salvaged goods at a discount. He offered an assortment of all kinds of bargain products—from food, hardware, and clothes to daily necessities like toothbrushes and razors. Whenever he heard that a store was going out of

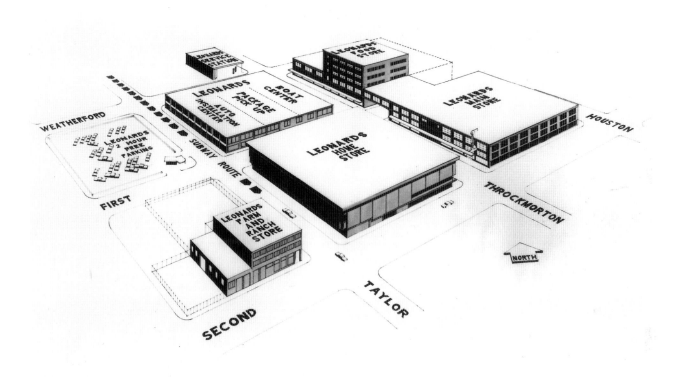

Drawing of the eventual seven-block location of Leonard Brothers.
Courtesy of the Leonard Store Museum.

The Leonard brothers created many innovations, such as the first baby strollers any company offered for customers with young children. Marvin had seen many a woman walk through the store with a baby or two in her arms. How could she examine any merchandise? After discussing this dilemma with his brother, Obie developed a rolling stroller with a seat up front where a child could sit, and a compartment in the back to hold the products the mother wished to purchase. Leonard Brothers also introduced a Christmas Toyland for children that would rival Manhattan's Macy's. There the kids could

Obie and Marvin Leonard admiring their
department store empire in downtown
Fort Worth in the late 1960s.
Courtesy of Marty Leonard.

explore Santa's fantasyland, which included lights, trains, and mythical scenes and characters of yuletide. There was a monorail in the ceiling that encircled Toyland and enthralled both children and adults.

Leonard Brothers also installed the first escalator west of the Mississippi after Obie designed and help engineer their own version of the mechanical customer-moving device. Because parking was at a minimum in downtown Fort Worth, Marvin and Obie created a bus shuttle system from a parking lot they owned near the Trinity River, about a mile from downtown. Always seeking to improve service, they upgraded the shuttle in 1963 when they completed the first underground subway system in Texas, and the only privately owned subway in the world. The train's route ended in the basement of Leonard Brothers. As Marvin said after construction was completed, "To get to any business in downtown Fort Worth, the folks have to come through our store."

When they expanded in the 1930s, the brothers decided their old location would be perfect for products they could sell at the deepest discounts, and so they created a location called "Everybody's." This location catered to lower-income families who were struggling through the Great Depression, and it continued to operate until Leonard Brothers was sold to Tandy Corporation in the 1970s.

"My father and my uncle were both incredibly ingenious, generous, and as different as they could be," Marty Leonard offered. "Uncle Obie, well, he was a character, a very different personality from my father. I mean their way of life was very different. Daddy went the golf route, you know, drinking and gambling, and doing those kinds of things; and that was as far from Obie as anything could be. Obie was involved in hunting, fishing, ranching, and farming. I loved them both."

By 1927, sales at Leonard Brothers exceeded one million dollars. During those first eight years, Marvin had invested his personal earnings from the store in banking, oil, and real estate deals, and had become a wealthy, respected citizen of Fort Worth.

His success came at a price. Marvin had worked extremely hard, long hours to achieve his goals, and in the spring of 1927, a doctor examining him told Marvin his health was not as good as it should be. He needed to take a break from the stress of work. Suggesting some activity outdoors that would be healthy and good for him, the doctor asked, "Why don't you try golf?" Marvin thought for a moment, and then responded, "Okay, I'll give it a try."

Marvin selected Glen Garden Golf and Country Club as his preferred site for learning the game. He almost quit after the first day, thinking that chasing the little white ball might not be for him. But Marvin came back to Glen Garden and gave it another chance. He became a respectable golfer, and soon afterward fell in love with the game. He would go to the club several times each week, arrive early, play nine holes, and then go to work. As was the custom in those days at Glen Garden Golf and Country Club, all members used caddies.

JACQUE: *When he was a young teenager, Uncle Ben rose early to get in line to caddy before the other caddies arrived. There were times when he would go out to Glen Garden in the late afternoon after he had sold all but a couple of his newspapers at the T&P station. He would lay one newspaper in a sand trap and lie down on it, and cover himself with another newspaper. He would sleep in the trap so that he could be the first in line at the caddy shack the next morning. And—it had to be fate—one early morning Uncle Ben met Mr. Leonard and started caddying for him.*

The meeting of Marvin Leonard and the Hogan boys was kismet, and it was the beginning of a lifetime friendship among the three of them. Although Royal and Ben were dirt poor, and Marvin, also from humble beginnings, was on his way to becoming a very wealthy man, there was something that attracted each to the other.

JACQUE: *For my father, the value in their relationship was an exposure to success in business, and for Uncle Ben, Marvin was the father figure he had missed so much. And for Marvin, perhaps it was like having a son. Marvin's four children all turned out to be girls, and one of them, Marty, is a good friend of mine. The girls were a delight to Marvin, but having someone he could be with who was like a son was very special. Between Uncle Ben and Marvin it was golf, and later, investments. For Daddy and Marvin, it was sharing a mutual respect for business and similar work ethics. I really liked Mr. Leonard, who everyone called "Mr. Marvin." He used to call me "Little Hogan."*

After Ben had been caddying for Marvin for a couple of years, they started playing together as well. During those early years, Ben and Marvin forged the strongest bonds of mutual respect and friendship. Marvin became Ben's strongest supporter; one today might call him a sponsor. During those lean years on the PGA tour, when Ben was working as an underpaid club pro, Marvin bailed the couple out more than once when Ben and Valerie ran out of money on the road. On several occasions Marvin wired two or three hundred dollars to help them get to the next series of tournaments or to return home. Later, after Ben had success on the tour, he repeatedly tried to pay back those financial advances, but Marvin would never take the money. He told the young Mr. Hogan, "Ben, all I wanted to know is that you *wanted* to pay it back."

Marvin had developed a serious golf "bug," and played every day he could. Eventually he joined River Crest Country Club on the west side, in addition to Glen Garden. He also started to travel around and play other courses, because he was becoming interested in course layout and design. He began to entertain the idea of building a golf course combined with a residential development.

In 1931, Marvin Leonard married Mary Elinore Vaughan, and they honeymooned in New York City. Marvin couldn't help but use the time they stayed in Manhattan to shop for deals and purchase products for resale at Leonard Brothers.

Marvin and Mary loved to vacation on the Monterrey Peninsula, where Marvin could play golf at Pebble Beach and the other excellent courses in the area. Marvin had grown to love the bentgrass greens that carpeted West Coast courses, as opposed to the Bermuda grass greens used in the hot, humid South. It was always thought that bentgrass couldn't survive the Texas heat, but Marvin began to believe that a strain named "Seaside," which was developed in Coos Bay, Oregon, might work in Fort Worth. He felt that it would

work if he secured enough of a water supply to keep the greens cooled down. After returning from his vacation, Marvin approached the board of River Crest and asked them if they might change three or four of the greens to bentgrass. They declined. He persisted and offered to pay for the transformation to bentgrass and back to Bermuda if it failed, but again the members of the club rebuffed his offer. They basically told Marvin that if he wanted to experiment with a grass that couldn't grow in Texas, then he should build his own damn golf course, for he wasn't going to get any cooperation from River Crest.

Marvin had purchased a couple hundred acres on the west fork of the Trinity River, just inside the Fort Worth city limits, in the 1930s. He began to envision a golf course and a residential development on this land. The ample amount of water from the location near the Trinity was the answer to the problem of the bentgrass dilemma. Whether it was Marvin's natural determination or plain Texas bullheadedness, he made the decision to follow through on his vision.

He brought in golf course designer John Bredemus to help with the layout and construction of what Marvin hoped would be a championship course, one that could make Fort Worth proud. He also hired the architectural firm of Hare & Hare to help develop a residential neighborhood which would be adjacent to the golf course. Marvin wanted a golf course that was contained within boundaries, and not wandering through the neighborhood. The Depression was in full swing, and the construction of the golf course and the neighborhood, to be known as Colonial Hills, provided hundreds of jobs for the needy folks of Fort Worth. One individual, a high school senior named Joe Cano, got a job cutting down trees, clearing fields, and moving dirt from one location to another around the layout for the construction of the greens. Joe continued to work for Mr. Marvin and eventually became the greens keeper once the course was completed. On January 29, 1936, the unmatched Colonial Country Club, complete with eighteen bentgrass greens, opened with one hundred members, including the Hogan brothers, and one proud owner, Marvin Leonard.

Colonial Country Club opened in 1936 with a magnificent colonial-style clubhouse and lockers for 250 men and women members, who paid a fifty-dollar deposit fee and dues of ten dollars a month. At first, there were very few country club amenities other than the chance to play a new, top-rated golf course. It would be a couple of years before Marvin had the resources to add a pool, tennis courts, and a game room that had actual slot machines. Marvin continued to be the sole owner and president of the club for many years to follow, before he eventually sold it to its members.

As soon as the course opened the reviews flowed in, declaring Colonial to be a success and the first championship course in the state. No less than A. W. Tillinghast, a famous golf course architect and consultant to the Professional Golf Association (PGA), praised Colonial for its experiment with bentgrass greens and declared them much better than Bermuda. Marvin began to hope that one year soon, the club could host a yearly tournament to challenge the talents of professionals and amateurs alike. For the next few years, the club course hosted various tournaments: men's, women's, pros', amateurs'. These included the Fort Worth Women's Open, Texas Women's Open, Texas PGA, and many memorable cup matches and exhibitions.

In 1939, Dr. Alden Coffey, a respected Fort Worth physician, and newspaper publisher Amon Carter Sr., a good friend of Marvin's, convinced him and other Fort Worth businessmen that the city should attempt to bring the US Open to the club. Marvin went to work, attempting to convince the United States Golf Association (USGA) to host the National Open Championship at Colonial.

Up until then, all course venues for the US Open Championship had been played north of the Mason-Dixon line and east of the Mississippi, with the single exception of Cherry Hills Country Club in Denver, in 1938. After committee members of the USGA had inspected and played Fort Worth's magnificent layout, on May 8, 1940, the board voted for Colonial to host the 1941 National Open Championship. There were a few caveats with the announcement. Though they had already signed off on Colonial as the site for the 1941 Open, after more USGA board members visited the course, it was determined that the fourth hole was unacceptable and would have to be upgraded. The USGA gave Colonial about three hundred days to get the course prepared properly for the national championship, or they would relocate the 1941 event to Merion, Oakmont, Inverness, Olympia Fields, Baltusrol, or Oakland Hills, all of which were courses that had hosted multiple Opens over the years. Marvin brought in Perry Maxwell, a famous golf architect from Tulsa, to oversee the redesign of the fourth hole. He wanted the new number four to be a 240-yard par three, but in order to do so he would need to redesign numbers three and five, as well, and there wasn't really enough room. This required Mr. Leonard to purchase some land adjacent to the old numbers four and five, which was a forest by the river. Crews cleared the forest, built a completely new fifth hole, and rebuilt three and four. The new three, four, and five holes, now

known very affectionately as "The Horrible Horseshoe," became the most famous and difficult section of Colonial. After only nine months the three holes were complete, and the USGA determined Colonial was ready to host the best golfers in the world.

One final gesture assured the USGA that the event would not lose money. Earl Collins, a later neighbor of Royal Hogan's and a long-time Colonial Country Club member, recalled, "It was the first time the Open would be played in the South, and the USGA was afraid the event wouldn't be able to draw enough people to make it pay for itself. I was told Mr. Leonard called the offices of the USGA. He was talking for quite awhile with one of the directors, who finally said, 'Mr. Leonard, this is getting to be a pretty expensive phone call.' And Mr. Leonard, said, 'I don't care; it's on my tab. Listen, I will guarantee you a $25,000 gate, and in case our Open doesn't draw large enough galleries, the balance will come out of my pocket.' In 1941, that was a pretty good chunk of money. But [the guarantee] worked. The director said, 'Well, okay.' And so the USGA came down to Fort Worth to run their national championship at Colonial."

Mr. Marvin's vision of hosting a major tournament at his beloved championship course along the banks of the Trinity River was fully realized.

6

FAMILY GOLF

oyal and Ben were among the first one hundred members to join Colonial. Up to this time, Royal was beating Ben regularly when they played together, and that challenge drove Ben to work even harder on his swing and his approach to the game. This was before golf coaches or physical trainers became popular, and many players had to figure their problems out for themselves. Ben told others that he learned the proper swing from watching the great players he had caddied for or later saw on the tour. Watching these great golfers had not helped cure his constant hook, however. Ben eventually found his "secret" in a new grip and a modified address to the ball that allowed him to play a soft fade that he could control. At the same time he was developing a dedication and commitment to the game that allowed for pure concentration, perfect focus, and planning.

ROBERT: *Ben told Jacque that his "secret" was more of a spiritual thing than a technical or physical adjustment. Golf, it turned out, fit perfectly with his nature. It was a game with defined rights and wrongs, much like life was for Mama Hogan. It was a game in which winning or losing depended upon one's own skills and was not supported by the skills of other teammates. Executing near perfection playing golf involved individual thought, concentration, dedication, and ex-*

ecution, all of which fit Ben's personality. He could be a terrific partner or team man when the format called for it, but he was otherwise a loner . . . and successful professional golf was a loner's game. Golf was (and is) a game that promotes fairness and imposes penalties on those who do not play by the rules. This suited Ben's honesty very well, as he had always said, "No one else would ever have to call a penalty on me because I would call it on myself."

As he worked harder and harder on his new technique, Ben developed into one of the very best, true ball strikers and shot makers the game has ever known. Royal was an early witness to this fact, as he began to realize that he was unable to beat Ben nearly as often as he had in earlier years. In fact, Royal was fast becoming one of his younger brother's biggest fans, and starting in 1939, he would take Margaret and Jacqueline with him to follow his younger brother on the tour.

JACQUE: *From the time I was about six years old, my daddy would take my mother and me to find Uncle Ben on the golf circuit every summer. As soon as school ended, we would board a train to Uncle Ben's next tournament. Once or twice we might have traveled by car, but most of the time we took the train. We'd have a sleeper compartment, with its own bathroom, and a couch that turned into a bed, and another bed that dropped*

Royal Hogan holds six-month-old Jacqueline.
JHT family collection.

down from the wall. During that period, the professional golfers didn't hopscotch all over everywhere. They went from one tournament to the next, and they had them all bunched up close together, usually no more than a one-day drive apart. You didn't have to go

Margaret Hogan with six-month-old Jacqueline.
JHT family collection.

from the East Coast to the West Coast, or from the West Coast down to Florida. Most of my early summers, the tournaments were in New York state, Pennsylvania, or Illinois. So, that was our vacation—following Uncle Ben on the golf tour somewhere in the East.

Traveling in first-class sleeper compartments, Royal and his family enjoyed the ben-

efits of the luxurious train travel of the day, including excellent service from men in white jackets. "They had some of the best food you could eat," as Jacque described it. The entire experience was exciting for young Jacqueline. Once they reached their destination, the family would stay in the finest hotels with room service and fine dining rooms. Occasionally, they would dine with Ben, but only when he was between events.

JACQUE: *We would see Uncle Ben on the course. He didn't socialize during golf tournaments. It was all business. He would play his round and then he would practice on the range. Then, he would return to his hotel room. But instead of relaxing, he would continue to practice. I remember the management of several hotels had to come to his room and say, "Mr. Hogan, would you please quit hitting golf balls against the walls." Uncle Ben was very strategic in planning for a tournament. He had a marvelous memory, which suited his strategy very well. He memorized every feature of each hole of the course, planning the paths he wanted to follow during the tournament, especially his chosen angle from which to approach the greens.*

ROBERT: *Ben would study various lies [landing areas] at which he wanted to aim his shots. In a practice round he would hit three balls to different places on the fairway, testing the wind, the slopes, and the location of preferred landing areas. When he approached the green, he would turn and look back at the layout of the hole and map the best path to the green. He literally knew what shot he was going to make on each hole under any condition, and because he practiced all of the shots during a practice round, he would not be surprised by any shot required of him during the tournament. What other golfer has ever played with such mental commitment and strategic planning? Maybe Nicklaus came close, but no one could really challenge Ben's preparation for managing a round of golf.*

Royal would spend these "vacations" mixing leisure, golf, and work. If he knew a manufacturer of products he was distributing was located nearby, he would take Margaret and little Jacqueline with him to call on the factory.

JACQUE: *I remember how wonderful it was that Daddy would take us to these companies, where we would see how they made the pencils, pens, or chairs. I was amazed how they could make these things by hand. It was incredible. I'll never forget the lady at Wallace Pencils in St. Louis, who could reach into a large container and pull out exactly twelve pencils every time and set them in a pencil box. Every time, she took out twelve. I watched her for a long time—always twelve pencils! That was amazing.*

Royal loved to know the ins and outs of

Signed to "Mr. and Mrs. Hogan" (Royal and Margaret), from Ben Hogan. JHT family collection.

all of the products he sold, and firsthand knowledge was of the utmost importance to him. Occasionally, he would call his store to check in, but he trusted his employees to look after the business while he was away.

JACQUE: *Daddy loved golf so much, and he truly enjoyed following Uncle Ben on the*

Royal Hogan, wearing his daughter Jacqueline's stocking cap, prepares to play Glen Garden Golf and Country Club on a cold winter day. In the background is the caddy shack where Royal and Ben worked as youngsters.
JHT family collection.

circuit. I learned these were the rare times Daddy looked as if he was releasing control of his business. But trust me, somehow he was always aware of what was happening back at the store.

At the end of every summer, Royal would take the family with him as he competed in one of the premiere amateur golf tournaments, the Broadmoor Invitational in Colorado Springs. This esteemed annual event was first played in 1921 and continued until 1994.

JACQUE: *My mother was afraid to fly. One year we took a plane to Colorado Springs, but she refused to fly back, and we had to find another way home. I believe that was the last time my mother ever got on an airplane. Daddy loved playing at the Broadmoor, so we continued to go every August. Usually, we stayed at the Broadmoor resort. One year Daddy enjoyed the good graces of a friend, Neville Penrose, from Fort Worth, who had this wonderful cabin high up on the mountain above the resort. He told Daddy we could have it for the week of the tournament. Daddy was so excited about it, but oh God, my mother hated it. It was rustic and it was up on a mountain! She couldn't stand the fact that there was no room service, no restaurants, and she had to cook. She had always had a cook at home. After two days,*

Front view of the Hogans' Alton Road house in 1941. JHT family collection.

she was so distressed we moved back to the Broadmoor.

In March of 1940, Ben won his first professional individual tournament at the Pinehurst, North Carolina's North and South Open. Once Ben Hogan was off the schneid, it was Katy bar the door. He quickly added to his first win with victories the next two weeks at the Greensboro Open and the Asheville Open. He finished out the year winning $10,656, making him the top money winner on the tour. It was by far his most successful year to date. Comparable wins in today's televised worldwide games would fetch in the neighborhood of $3,500,000.

In 1941, Royal decided he wanted to live

Jacqueline Hogan checks the mail in front
of the Alton Road house.
JHT family collection.

build the house on Alton Road, with the TCU football stadium practically in our backyard. Just like he did with his business loan, he paid off the loan on the house in six months and never again borrowed money for anything. Living and working through the Depression had a deep impact on my daddy, as it did many others. He never trusted the banks and always kept a large amount of cash in his office safe. A few years after we moved to Alton Road, my uncle and Aunt Princess moved in practically across the street. They would drink coffee and smoke cigarettes all day, every day, for as long as I knew them. But they were both a delight to be around. Princess always had an Elberta peach tree in her backyard, and people said you couldn't grow them in Fort Worth, but she did. Also, as I mentioned, she was a great cook, and made the best red velvet cake. The whole family loved it.

Every year my dad would drive out to Weatherford and buy a bushel of peaches. He would bring them home and peel each one personally and then make peach preserves for the family. With the remaining peaches, we would make homemade peach ice cream. My job was to sit on the top of ice cream maker while Daddy would crank it to produce the most delicious of treats. Uncle Ben absolutely loved it—he could eat four or five bowls. Those were fun family times.

closer to Colonial, and although he would remain a member at Glen Garden and other clubs around the area, Colonial would become his home course. Royal went on to be its club champion four times.

JACQUE: *For the second time in his life, Daddy borrowed money so that he could*

The Alton Road house was my home from the third grade until I went to college. From that home I attended Alice E. Carlson Elementary, then later McLean Junior High, and finally Paschal High School. That was where I first met Robert.

Jacque's future husband, Robert Towery, had met Jacque's father before the two of them knew each other in high school, and he learned firsthand how difficult and controlling Royal could be.

JACQUE: *Uncle Ben internalized whatever anger he had and he used it to push himself forward. A hint of this could be seen when he inhaled a cigarette, burning an inch off the weed in one breath. No one ever saw Ben Hogan throw a club in anger, and most people never saw my daddy throw a club. My husband Robert, however, was an exception. Robert Towery also caddied at Glen Garden when he was a youngster, walking from his home at 1032 East Jessamine in the Morningside neighborhood, about five miles from the golf course. Robert didn't have to go through the kangaroo court routine experienced by Ben and others years earlier, but he did have to work his way up the ladder of caddying. Newcomers were typically assigned to less talented and lower-paying golfers, but as one progressed up the ladder, the job provided better golfers and, usually, better tips.*

Robert moved up a level when he quali-fied to carry for two golfers, and he enjoyed the double pay and double tips. This advance usually meant no more singles. Eventually he was recognized as a first-rate caddy, and one day the caddy master asked him to caddy for a really good golfer who wanted his own caddy, meaning he would have no double for the day. Robert reluctantly agreed, and then he met his new golfer at the first tee—Royal Hogan. All went well during the initial round, and Robert really enjoyed caddying for such a talented golfer. Robert was surprised and disappointed when he received a ten-cent tip, however, as twenty-five cents was the usual tip for a good round. Robert knew that he could do better than that. The next time Royal played Glen Garden, Royal again requested Robert as his caddy.

The round was going well until the signature eighth hole, which required a tee shot over the lake to the dogleg fairway to the right on the other side.

JACQUE: *Robert said that my father hit his first ball into the lake. There was dead silence on the tee box until he turned to Robert and asked for another ball. Daddy hit his second ball into the lake, and then his driver followed. After the other players had teed off, Daddy turned to Robert and told him to fetch his driver from the lake. Robert replied that there were water moccasins in that water and he was afraid of snakes. My father insisted*

Colonial Country Club Champions with founder Marvin Leonard.
LEFT TO RIGHT: Rube Berry ('45, '46), J. J. ("Joe") Ballard Jr. ('39), Max Highfill ('38),
Marvin Leonard (he never won but once finished second), Johnny Ballard ('42), W. A. Moncrief ('40)
and Royal Hogan ('44, '48, '49, '53). Courtesy of Colonial Country Club, Fort Worth, Texas.

that Robert go into the lake and retrieve the golf club, to which he replied, "No, sir!" My daddy then told him to either go retrieve the club or return to the clubhouse. So, Robert did just that, returning to the caddy shack. The next day he learned he was no longer a caddy at Glen Garden. Daddy had him fired!

Don Matheson, who attended the University of Oklahoma on a golf scholarship, was born five blocks from Colonial Country Club. As a teenager, Don played Colonial regularly, but never played with Royal Hogan, although he wished he could have. His regular group included Jimmy Wilson, John Ballard, and Dan Greenwood.

Don recalled, "At Colonial, Royal played with Rube Berry, Rudy Copeland, Joe Ballard, Pete Donough, Ernie Vossler, Don Cherry— all really good golfers. They liked to gamble. We gambled in our regular game, but our bets were peanuts compared to Royal and his cronies, who played high-stakes matches. Playing golf in college, all of us golfers worshipped Ben Hogan, but he was very private, not receptive to talking to anyone while he was practicing. But he let me and a couple of other young golfers watch him from a distance. He knew we were there, but he never paid attention to us."

Jerre Todd was a sportswriter with the *Fort Worth Press*, on a staff with Dan Jenkins and Bud Shrake, all of them under the

Royal and nine-year-old Jacqueline as Royal competed for his third City Championship.
Courtesy of FWST/UTA.

guidance of the legendary Blackie Sherrod. Jerre related, "We covered all sports. We went to work at six in the morning and you had to write ten or eleven stories before the eight o'clock deadline. So, we'd just blow 'em out. No time to ever check the facts. We would clip the box score out of the morning *Star-Telegram* and have it typeset. The *Star-Telegram* caught on to that, and they would intentionally place errors in the morning box score to catch us. They were trying to make us look bad, because we were doing the same thing they were."

The *Press* started in 1921 and closed in the 1970s. It was always an afternoon paper. It had a circulation of about 45,000, whereas the *Star-Telegram* had 220,000 readers. Jerre recalled the gamesmanship with their rival newspaper. "Amon Carter, the owner of the *Star-Telegram*, was a crusty old man—and very competitive. He would see Leonard's or Hogan's advertisements in the *Press* and he would call them up and tell them they were wasting their money."

"Ben wasn't nearly as distant and aloof as his reputation described," Jerre recalled. "He was shy, you know. I'm sure Royal was, too. Royal was an extremely competitive golfer. He would cut off his foot to win a match, and he was a great putter."

Another Colonial member, Cecil Morgan Jr., started playing at the club when he was twelve years old. His father was a charter member at Colonial. After Cecil left the armed service, he spent four years working with an oil company, then relocated to Fort Worth to become an investment broker. Cecil likes to tell the story about his father joining Colonial, "Marvin Leonard approached my father one day, and said, 'Cecil, I want you to join the club.'"

"Mr. Marvin," Cecil said, "I can't afford it. I just started a law practice."

Marvin whispered, "I'm only talking about $50. If you move or can't afford it, I'll give you your money back."

Cecil recalled, "Mr. Marvin was a great man . . . and, besides creating Colonial and Shady Oaks, he built the best nine-hole golf course ever out at Starr Hollow."

Cecil loved to watch Royal and Ben play golf. "When we were twenty-five to thirty," he remembered, "we were all intimidated by Royal on the golf course. He dressed like Ben, looked like Ben—perhaps a little taller, but strikingly similar. He was an impressive ball striker."

Over the years, the comedian Bob Hope played several rounds of golf with the Hogan brothers, and, as luck would have it, with Cecil Morgan Sr. Cecil Jr. recalled Bob Hope joking during a round: "When a baby's born in Texas, the doctor turns him upside down, slaps his butt, and says, 'What's your handicap?'"

7

"THIS THING IS LEGENDARY"

In 1896, a Fort Worth area rancher named Charles McFarland and the marketing manager for the Fort Worth Stockyards, Charles French, were talking about the growing cattle business in Cowtown, and they came up with the concept of a stock show. The inaugural event involved a handful of ranchers, exhibitors, and organizers showing off their stock in an open field by Marine Creek. Since it began 118 years ago, the stock show has grown into the largest annual event in Fort Worth, drawing over one million visitors each year. The stock show is incorporated as a non-profit organization which has used the large amounts of money it has generated over the years to provide grants for Ranch Management at TCU and agricultur-al experimentation at Texas Tech, as well as scholarships for veterinarian students at Texas A&M.

Since its inception, the Fort Worth Stock Show has undergone numerous name changes, and there have been many firsts along the way. The initial stock show had a parade that opened the event and ran north up Main Street to the courthouse, and then back down Houston Street toward the south. The tradition of the parade opening the stock show has endured to present days. In 1918, the stock show added a rodeo. Held at the Northside Coliseum, it was the first indoor rodeo in the world. With that addition, the event became known as the Fort Worth Stock Show and Rodeo, and starting in the 1920s, Verne

Elliot, producer of the rodeo, created many innovations and new events. Verne Elliot had been riding in rodeos for years before becoming a producer of the Calgary Stampede, and had produced rodeos in Denver, Chicago, Phoenix, and Kansas City before he came to Fort Worth. Elliot and his partners initiated Brahman bull riding in 1920. In 1927, Elliott added bareback bronc riding and introduced side-releasing bucking chutes, which rodeos everywhere continue to use today. Other firsts included 1932's first live radio broadcast of a rodeo by NBC, utilizing Amon Carter's Fort Worth affiliate, WBAP. In 1944, the stock show moved into the Will Rogers Memorial Center and introduced intermission entertainment, a staple in most rodeos today. In an effort to get off to a stellar start, the producers engaged Gene Autry, the singing cowboy, as their first entertainer. Then in 1958, with guest stars Roy Rogers and Dale Evans as the hosts, NBC-TV aired the entire rodeo live to homes across the nation.

JACQUE: *When I was seven years old, my childhood friend Joy Crowder and I had horses that we rode almost daily at Forest Park. We were invited to ride in the parade leading up to the stock show and rodeo, and we continued to participate for several years. It is the only parade not using motorized vehicles, only animals such as horses, mules, and donkeys to propel the wagons and floats. Joy and I also rode in the Grand Entry that opened each rodeo. One year, she almost got me killed. She told me she had a friend who had offered two horses for us to ride in the Grand Entry. After waiting in the wings, as the flag bearers on horses positioned themselves around the arena, we entered at full gallop. We would race down the right side of the arena, turn sharply to the left at the other end, and ride figure eights around the flag bearers on the way to our exit. Joy failed to mention I was riding a trained cutting horse, so when I pulled the reins left, that cutting horse turned immediately, on a dime, and I was propelled out of the saddle in the direction of the barrier. At the last second, I grabbed the reins, the mane, the saddle horn, and anything else I could, to stay on that horse. I could have been killed. But I wasn't. And I didn't hold it against my friend for very long. Every year, Joy and I also showed our horses in competition during the rodeo. We competed in the Western Saddle Class, where we trotted, walked, and made exact turns, all under the watchful eyes of the judges. My horse, Suzy, was a wonderful competitor, and I participated every year until the flood of 1949. The overflowing waters of the Trinity River forced the owners of the stables where I boarded Suzy, across from the fifth tee at Colonial, to let out all of the horses. Suzy was carried downstream. She survived, but was cut up pretty bad, and I couldn't show her in competition anymore.*

Another childhood friend of Jacqueline's was Marianne Hannon. The Hannons had the first house on Alton Road; the Hogans built the second. Marianne and Jacqueline were fast friends from the beginning.

JACQUE: *Marianne's mother was named Wannabea, but everyone called her Bea. She was a great cook, and she and my mother were good friends. Both Bea and my mother were very private by nature, which was one of the reasons they were so close.*

Marianne recalls, "I loved Jacque's mother when I was a child. She was wonderful, kind, and always very nice to me. I remember Mother and Margaret would sit on the porch in the afternoons, sharing a beer and watching us play in the yard. Jacque and I played together in those elementary school days, but rarely included other children. During those days we were pretty much forbidden to play with other people because of the fear of acquiring polio through interaction with an infected child."

JACQUE: *Yes. Polio was an epidemic, and our mothers had a great fear we might contract the disease. I was in college before they came up with the vaccine. As we got older, though, we did start to socialize with others and began to hang out at the swimming pool at Colonial.*

Marianne remembers, "Jacque and I were inseparable from the time we first met. When

Royal Hogan and son Royal Dean, with Dr. Howard Ditto, on the way to the world famous Fort Worth Stock Show and Rodeo in 1955. JHT family collection.

we were fourteen years old, our parents packed us off to camp together."

JACQUE: *In those days almost all the Fort Worth girls who attended camp went to Camp Waldemar in Hunt, Texas, near the headwaters of the beautiful Guadalupe River. I hated the idea of going to camp at first, but once*

I was there, I grew to love it. I learned the art of Roman-style riding at Camp Waldemar, where I could ride two horses standing on their bare backs. The camp was separated into three tribes, formed for friendly camp competitions. When we arrived at camp, we would draw out of a large box the name of the tribe we were to join. Each tribe had a color designation. Marianne and I drew the card for the Comanche tribe, which was designated with the color orange. The other two tribes were the Aztecs, represented by green, and the Tejas team, which was purple.

All of the tribes shared breakfast, lunch, and dinner together in the dining hall built by a German stonemason named Ferdinand Rehberger. He constructed the majestic three-story structure with honeycomb rock, a type of limestone he found near the Guadalupe River. The interior resembles a massive cave wall, and Rehberger's work was so precise it is difficult to find the seams between the rocks. Overseeing the junior and senior dining halls were the Waldemar chefs, and the two who stood out for their longevity, recipes, loyalty, and love for the camp were Lucille and U. S. Smith.

JACQUE: *Lucille and her husband were the chefs at Camp Waldemar for nearly fifty years. She was a wonderful cook and a tremendous baker. She made the most delicious fried chicken, hot rolls, doughnuts, corn-bread, and homemade vanilla ice cream ever. Every day she would make us an afternoon snack like chocolate chip cookies that were to die for.*

U. S. was known for his barbecue skills and was celebrated as the "Barbecue King of the Southwest" while catering for W. T. Johnson's traveling rodeo. He was a large man who commanded respect, always wearing a tall chef's hat and a starched, pristine white chef's coat. Lucille was a legend in her own right. She was recognized as one of the top one hundred women of the twentieth century in Texas. In addition to her duties at Camp Waldemar, she was noted for creating the first packaged bread mix for the marketplace, "Lucille's Hot Roll Mix," an early version of the prepackaged mixes and other kinds of baking shortcuts taken for granted today. The excellent array of meals prepared by Lucille and U. S. was served family style, and the campers learned proper manners and table etiquette during these delicious feasts.

JACQUE: *When we weren't eating the fabulous food, there were all types of activities to keep us busy, like archery, swimming, diving, horseback riding, and War Canoe, which consisted of ten paddles in a long canoe, five to a side, with another camper, the coxswain, at the back steering the canoe. Every session at Camp Waldemar ended with the Field Days competitions, and the War Canoe races were the most fun of all the events, with the winning tribe holding bragging rights until the next term. I made War Canoe. It was a big honor. Out of the sixty members of a tribe, only eleven were chosen. We had to try out, and once we made the team, we had to practice really hard. We took it very seriously.*

"Oh, yes," Marianne added, "War Canoe was the big event at Field Days, and if I remember correctly, the Comanches were victorious our first year."

JACQUE: *Putting a nice touch to the end of camp that year, my father brought me my first car—a black Mercury convertible, and I really loved it. I didn't have a license, so Daddy drove us home. Naturally, I got my driver's license as soon as I returned to Fort Worth.*

Marianne remembered a different kind of camp event involving the two Fort Worth girls. "A couple of years after Camp Waldemar, Jacque and I went to a Camp Fire Girls camp outside of Granbury, not very far from Fort Worth. The 220-acre, multiuse camp was known as El Tesoro and had been in existence since 1913. We were there for about ten days. Somehow, our mothers found out that we didn't have any candy or sweets. Jacque's mom, Margaret, and my mother snuck across a creek in the middle of the night, and brought us a care package."

JACQUE: *My mother actually walked across a creek, dressed to the nines like always, and to top it off, did it in high heels. I couldn't believe she really did that.*

Joy Crowder recalled, "Mrs. Hogan was a tiny, really fashionable lady. Perfectly manicured, color coordinated. We loved to go shopping with her, she was so stylish, and she took us to all the best stores. On the other hand, Jacque's father was very secretive. I never really got to know Mr. Hogan. Except the one time he took Jacque, me, and our dates to Arlington Downs for the horse races. He seemed to loosen up a little. That was a ton of fun."

JACQUE: *Daddy loved the horse races.*

During those teenage years, Jacqueline, Joy, Marianne, and their other friends would hang out at the Colonial swimming pool when the sun was high and warming the water. Anyone who knows the Colonial environment can easily envision what a social hot spot it was, and still is.

JACQUE: *Mother very rarely came to the club. She was shy—introverted—and didn't like to socialize. She would be there on Easter, Thanksgiving, a few of the holidays for dinner, but that was it. Otherwise, she was never at Colonial.*

On weekend evenings, Joy, Jacqueline, and their dates would invariably end up at the Casino Park and Ballroom on the shores of Lake Worth, a few miles northwest of the city

LEFT TO RIGHT: Jacqueline Hogan, Martin Moore,
Bruce Pike, and Lois Ann Ward at a TCU party.
JHT family collection.

Paschal High School beauties: Front row, seated, left to right: Kathryn Minter, Marianne Hannon, Lura Elliston. Second row, standing, left to right: Mary L Spencer, Joy Crowder, Theresa Carroll, Jacqueline Hogan. Taken at a sorority party at Colonial Country Club. JHT family collection.

Royal Dean's second birthday party.
Left to right, back row: Princess and Howard Ditto,
Myrtle Duncan, Margaret Hogan, Mama Hogan,
and Royal Dean's nurse Joyce. Standing over
Royal Dean are Jacqueline and Royal Hogan.
JHT family collection

Jacqueline Hogan's graduation picture,
Paschal High School, 1951.
JHT family collection.

on Jacksboro Highway. The Casino Ballroom was a very long building with a huge circular mirrored ball reflecting light around the area as it spun above the dance floor. There was a large stage on one side, and plenty of room for dancing to the various Big Bands that would perform there each week. The entertainers and bands included Count Basie, Louis Armstrong, Duke Ellington, Tommy Dorsey, Glenn Miller, Frank Sinatra, and Rudy Vallee.

Joy recalled, "There was a liquor store outside the entrance to the Casino, where our dates would purchase vodka. At our table in the Casino, we would mix the vodka with 7-Up or cherry Cokes. I don't know how we managed that, but we did, and we never got sick."

"We were pretty wild in those days," Jacque admitted, "but we never got into trouble." When Jacqueline was nearing the end of high school, her father was approached by members of Steeplechase Club, who told him they wanted to present her debut to Fort Worth society. Steeplechase and another group called the Assembly both presented high school seniors to high society each year. The Assembly was made up of members of the "Fort Worth 400"—families of great wealth and distinction, although to be sure,

Jacqueline Hogan plays with Royal Dean Jr. in front of the family's first television set, Christmas 1952. JHT family collection.

being presented as a debutante by the men of Steeplechase also carried social status.

To the absolute surprise of the members of Steeplechase, Royal told them that his daughter would not be participating. It was the first time anyone had refused an offer for their daughter to be presented by the organization. Steeplechase persisted, stating that Jacque would make a wonderful addition to the season, but Royal refused again.

JACQUE: *When I heard Steeplechase Club wanted to present me to Fort Worth society, I was really honored. I approached my father to ask why he had turned them down. Daddy said, "You can't do that. Positively no!" I don't know if he felt it was too expensive or he might lose some control. It really hurt my feelings, and at the time, I thought it was a real slap in the face.*

Jacque was determined to attend TCU after high school. She had become engaged to a boy who was a cheerleader at TCU. Unfortunately, her father didn't like this boy's family–and again Jacque didn't know why.

JACQUE: *We lived right behind TCU at the time. I was engaged to a really great guy, but my father couldn't see it. To make certain I didn't marry him, Daddy approached me one day and said, "You're applying to SMU." That was that. I would attend college at SMU in Dallas.*

Despite the controlling aspects of her father's treatment of Jacque, which she grew to despise, she experienced a happy childhood spent with several girls who became lifelong friends. Her favorite memories growing up in Fort Worth include riding in the stock show parade, showing her horse Suzy during the rodeo competitions, the wonderful feasts at Camp Waldemar, swimming at Colonial, dancing at the Casino, and traveling to follow her beloved uncle on the professional golf tour.

Housekeeper Frances Jones,
with young Royal Dean Hogan Jr.
JHT family collection.

Royal Dean Hogan Jr., three years old.
Photo by Rhea-Engert..

8

THE WAR YEARS

The first couple of years during the 1940s were especially good times for the Hogan brothers. Royal's business was booming, and Ben was winning tournaments. Ben Hogan had paired with Vic Ghezzi to win a team four-ball tournament in 1938 at Hershey, but it was his tenth year on the tour in 1940 before he won his first individual title. As the 1940 professional circuit ended, Ben captured for the first time the Vardon Trophy, for having the lowest stroke average on the tour.

In 1941, the Hershey Country Club in Pennsylvania asked Ben to become their club pro and to represent them on the PGA tour, an association that would last for many years.

Most professionals on the tour represented one club or another around the country, because it was good publicity for a club to be associated with a player of championship caliber. It helped the professionals as well, because the club helped pay the expenses of playing on the tour. For about $8,000 a year, Ben's responsibilities included representing the candy company on the PGA circuit, and he was occasionally asked to play with some of the club members when he was at Hershey. He would, although he refused to play with merely average golfers, because he always wanted a challenge when he played rounds. Most of the time at the club, Ben could be found on the practice tee, hitting balls one after another. It wasn't unusual for him to practice in front of a small gallery made up of the Hershey club's members. From time to time, Ben would socialize with various members to further fulfill his duties as the club's pro.

JACQUE: *Uncle Ben had said privately that the Hershey deal made Valerie content, and this made it easier for him to concentrate solely on golf.*

On the tour in 1941, Ben continued his outstanding play, winning three more tournaments in Asheville, Chicago, and Hershey, and he finished in the money in every tournament he entered. He was beginning to be feared on the golf course by his competitors as he took home the Vardon Trophy again and earned top money for the second year in a row, with a record total of $18,358. His secret was apparently working.

Surprisingly, Ben's biggest disappointment in 1941 came at the US Open, played on his home course, Colonial. The previous year Ben had lowered his Colonial course record to 65, and he was favored, along with fellow Fort Worth native Byron Nelson, to win in 1941. The weather had been hot and almost perfect during the practice rounds, but the first two rounds were affected by adverse weather. On Friday, day two of the event, two huge thunderstorms stopped play for quite a while, and when it resumed the players were competing in what some golfers called a

The cover of the menu at the dining room of Hershey Country Club in Hershey, Pennsylvania. The club used this cover from the 1940s into the 1990s. JHT family collection.

"quagmire." After his second round, Byron Nelson remarked that putting on the number four green "was like putting on waves."

Cecil Morgan, a longtime member of the club whose father was a charter member at Colonial, recalled the deluge. "I was ten years old and a huge Ben Hogan fan. I remember it was raining really hard all day, and I made my little sister slog through the muck following Mr. Hogan for the whole eighteen holes. I don't think she ever forgave me for that."

Ben, unfortunately, shot himself out of the tournament the first two days with scores of 74 and 77, to trail the leaders by seven strokes at the halfway point. Despite final rounds of 68 and 70 to close out the thirty-six-hole final day of the Open, Ben eventually lost to the champion Craig Wood by five strokes. Wood almost didn't play in the event because he had injured his back in an automobile accident earlier in the year, and with the deluge on Friday he wanted to quit. He was talked out of it by his playing partner, Tommy Armour. Ben was disappointed by the loss, and even more so when he realized that World War II would suspend the Open for several years to come.

Although the United States would not suffer the ravages experienced by countries in Europe and Asia, the bombing of Pearl Harbor and the subsequent declaration of war by President Roosevelt dramatically affected everyone's lives. The 1942 season was up in the air, since most golfers expected to enlist or be drafted. The 1942 Masters was one of a handful of tournaments played during the year, and ironically Ben Hogan and Byron Nelson, who had met as fifteen-year-olds in the Glen Garden Caddy Championship, were tied with scores of 280 after seventy-two grueling holes, forcing an eighteen-hole playoff the following day. Byron woke up very ill

that morning, and Ben offered to postpone the playoff for a day until he could recover. Bryon declined the generous offer and said he would force down a sandwich and be ready. With twenty-five tour professionals among the gallery witnessing the playoff, Byron was able to defeat Ben by one stroke.

JACQUE: *This time around, Mr. Nelson denied Uncle Ben a green jacket. And it would be nine long years before he would finally win at Augusta.*

War would soon interrupt everyone's lives, but before his enlistment into the Army Air Corps in 1942, Ben would play in nine more tournaments, winning six of them: the Los Angeles, San Francisco, North and South, Asheville, and Rochester Opens, and one other tournament that was the most important to Ben. At the beginning of the year the USGA, stating that golf was basically irrelevant in the midst of a war, suspended the US Open. But as summer approached, in an effort to aid war bond sales, the USGA joined forces with the Chicago District Golf Association and the PGA to hold a one-time-only event: the Hale America National Open at Ridgemoor Country Club in Chicago. Participants in the Hale America were qualifiers drawn from 1,600 golfers who had participated in sixty-nine local and fourteen sectional qualifiers, exactly like the US Open. The prestigious field included the best players in the world not serving in the armed services, including defending US Open champion Craig Wood, Masters champion Byron Nelson, Jimmy Demaret, Lloyd Mangrum, Horton Smith, Jug McSpaden, and Lawson Little. Of the tour's greatest players at that time, only Sam Snead could not compete because of his military duties. Ben was there, however, standing shoulder to shoulder with the game's greats. In the final round, Hogan was paired with the legendary Bobby Jones, who was on leave from the army to make a rare playing appearance for the war bond drive. Ben Hogan won the event, shooting a 17-under 271, defeating the second place Demaret by three strokes.

JACQUE: *At the end of his career, Uncle Ben was credited with winning four US Opens, but he always felt he had won five because of his victory over a stellar field in the 1942 Hale America Open. He received the identical gold medallion given to the National Open winner. Uncle Ben told me late in his life that he deserved recognition for winning five opens. The Hale America win would've recorded him having one more than Willie Anderson, Bobby Jones and Jack Nicklaus. It would also have given him the record for the most national championships. When the USGA named the US Open prize the Jack Nicklaus Medallion in 2012, my uncle probably rolled over in his grave. I feel the USGA slighted Willie Anderson, Bobby Jones, and*

Ben Hogan relaxes after shooting a ten-under par 62 to lead the 1942 Hale America Open.
AP Wire Photo.

especially my Uncle Ben. All of his life, Uncle Ben felt he won five Opens; he had the medals to prove it. Uncle Ben was very proud of this achievement, and near the end of his life he still felt deprived of that recognition.

Ben holding his beloved dog Duffer, who was given to him by his good friend George Coleman, with Royal Dean Jr. and Mama Hogan.
JHT family collection.

One of the tournaments Ben entered and didn't win in 1942 was the Seminole Invitational. The tournament still proved to be a fortuitous event, however, as Ben became reacquainted with oilman George Coleman, whom he had met several years before. Originally from Oklahoma, Coleman and his wife shared a stunning house located on the beautiful Donald Ross-designed golfing gem, the Seminole Country Club at Juno Beach, Florida.

JACQUE: *Uncle Ben and George Coleman really connected with each other, and it was the beginning of a close, lifelong friendship. Mr. Coleman gave Uncle Ben a miniature black poodle that he named Duffer. The dog was always in the house, and he slept on Uncle Ben's bed. When they left the house for anything, a trip, a party, anywhere, they would have a lady come sit with Duffer. He was Uncle Ben's favorite companion for many years, and he was always very grateful to his friend George Coleman for the gift. Before the tour each year, Uncle Ben would spend time at Mr. and Mrs. Coleman's Florida home while practicing at the Seminole Country Club in preparation for the Masters.*

For the abbreviated 1942 tour, Ben would have won the Vardon Trophy, had it been awarded, and he was the tour's top money earner with a total $13,143. But it would be three years before he would again compete professionally. Private Ben Hogan reported for duty with the Army Air Corps on March 25, 1943. His older brother Royal was exempt from the service because of his age, a daughter, and the fact that he ran a retail business that supplied the local armed service locations around Fort Worth. Ben entered the Army Air Corps so that he could be based at Tarrant Field, just northwest of Fort Worth. He told friends that this enabled him to be close to Valerie, but those who knew him well felt the real reason he entered the air corps was to confront a secret fear "head on."

JACQUE: *Uncle Ben didn't like heights; he had a slight fear of flying, and he was a little claustrophobic, so you put him in a plane and he was not in his comfort zone. Knowing this about his brother, Daddy was very surprised to learn he enlisted in the air corps over the navy, but Uncle Ben joked he couldn't see himself wearing blue. By the way, blue was Valerie's favorite color. Their whole house was blue and white. Uncle Ben's favorite color was red, something we had in common.*

After six weeks of basic training, Ben was granted leave to play in a Red Cross benefit with Bob Hope and his Tarrant Field commanding officer, Colonel David Hutchinson, who was in charge of flying instruction. The Red Cross event led to other things. From 1943 through 1945, the colonel continued to ask Ben to play golf exhibitions with him around the country to help sell war bonds, or to raise money for the USO, or the Red Cross, or various hospitals in need of funds to take care of the wounded soldiers coming home. The pairing of Ben and his commanding officer would turn out to be a lifesaver in Ben's near and distant future. In November 1943, Ben was promoted to the rank of second lieutenant and sent to Kilgore, Texas, for basic flying instruction. After several months, Second Lieutenant Hogan was armed with a flying certificate as a copilot for light aircraft. He was transferred to Tulsa to attend the Spartan School of Aerodynamics, where he received advanced training in preparation for becoming a flight instructor. The war ended before he ever began instruction, and in 1945 Ben was permanently furloughed with the rank of captain.

JACQUE: *The war years had been challenging times. There was cigarette, chocolate, and gas rationing. There were always war bond rallies going on. Because we were at war with Japan, ladies couldn't get silk hose. This was before nylons, of course. People would donate empty metal cans and their lead-lined iceboxes to the war department. I remember donating our bacon grease to the government, which used it in the making of ammunition.*

During Ben's last year in the service, the tour resumed without him, and Byron Nelson dominated the 1945 season, winning eighteen tournaments, including an incredible record of eleven in a row. He had become the "Lord" of the tour, and even though they were old friends, Ben was a bit rankled that somebody else was ruling the world of golf when he wasn't competing. So, true to his nature, Ben practiced hard for his return to the tour during the 1946 season. All of his hard work paid off. When he finally returned to the tour, he won an amazing thirteen events, including his first major, the PGA at Portland Country Club in Oregon. After the completion of his most successful year yet, Ben was

Group photo of the Hogan family during WWII.
LEFT TO RIGHT: Royal, Margaret, Myrtle and Harry Duncan,
Jacqueline, Princess Ditto, Valerie, Ben, and Clara.
Photo taken by Dr. Howard Ditto.
JHT family collection.

once again the most feared golfer on the tour, and the leading money winner with $42,556. One of the events Ben won was the initial Colonial National Invitational Tournament (NIT) that was hosted by Marvin Leonard in May of 1946. After the success of the 1941 US Open, Marvin had been waiting patiently for the war to end so he could continue to promote his championship layout into a regular tour stop.

ROBERT: *The official prize money for the first NIT was $15,000, the third largest that season, and they limited the field to invited golfers—twenty-five professionals and four amateurs. Mr. Leonard was a very innovative businessman, and he really expressed that characteristic in this tournament. Colonial was the first tournament to place leader boards strategically around the golf course and to use mobile player standards so spectators would know what golfers they were watching and what their scores were at the time. Furthermore, he may have been the first to rope off the galleries, not only providing a better crowd flow but also preserving the playing condition of the fairways. He improved spectator seating areas and built state-of-the-art concession stands. Mr. Leonard knew how to do things right, a trait shared by Jacque's Uncle Ben, and this may have been one reason Ben and Mr. Leonard got along so well.*

Ben and Royal were both in the field of their home course's first PGA event. Royal played as one of only four amateurs, and finished a disappointing twenty-fifth. His younger brother Ben would come from behind in the last round to win by one stroke—shooting a tournament course record of 65. This was the first of five victories for Ben at Marvin's tournament, and because of his dominance on his home course, Colonial be-

came known in the 1950s as Hogan's Alley. Riviera Country Club gave their course the same moniker, since Ben managed to win regularly at the Los Angeles layout, as well. Ben also won the Texas Open and the Dallas Open in 1946, and remains the only golfer to win three Texas events in the same year. He almost won the Texas Slam, but his old friend and nemesis Byron Nelson beat him by a single stroke in the Houston Open.

While Ben was dominating the professional field at Colonial, his brother Royal was doing a very respectable job against the amateurs. Royal won the Colonial Country Club Championship in 1944 and repeated in '48, '49, and '52. He also won the Fort Worth City Championship four times, causing great sports writer and Hogan friend Dan Jenkins to reflect, "Royal was a good local amateur player. I played a few rounds with him around Colonial. He won the City Championship—something Ben and Byron never did . . . or me. I remember Royal's setup and swing were remarkably similar to Ben's. I don't know who copied who, or whom, but I'm told Royal was the better player in their youth."

During the same period of time that Royal was dominating the local amateur events, Ben was crushing the competition at the Colonial NIT. Following his victory at the inaugural tournament hosted by Marvin Leonard,

Golfers and gallery at the 1946 Colonial National Invitational watch Ben Hogan sinking his final putt to seal his victory in the inaugural event.
Courtesy *FWST*/UTA.

Ben Hogan signs autographs for some of his youthful fans after winning the inaugural Colonial National Invitational Tournament in May of 1946. Notice the hat—this was before he switched to the style known as the Ivy, which was soon named after him. Courtesy of the Billy Wood Collection.

Amon Carter presents Ben Hogan a medal for winning the inaugural 1946 Colonial NIT. Courtesy of *FWST*/UTA.

Marvin Leonard presents Royal Hogan with the Leonard Trophy for winning the Colonial Country Club Championship in 1949. Courtesy of *FWST*/UTA.

Ben repeated as the champion in 1947, 1952, 1953, and even made it his last professional victory in 1959.

JACQUE: *I found it very interesting that my daddy's victories as club champion occurred roughly during the same time frame as Uncle Ben's championships in the Colonial Invitational. They were both at the top of their form during the same years.*

Ben continued to be hard to beat in 1947, as he won seven times and barely missed winning the Vardon Trophy again. He was second on the tour's top money list. It would be considered a very successful year by most golfers, but Ben was disheartened, as he didn't win the one major he dearly sought. In 1948, Ben rectified this when he entered the US Open at the Riviera Country Club. He shot a tournament record 276 and defeated Jimmy Demaret by one stroke.

It was during this period that Ben began to be referred to as the "Hawk." Jackie Burke, while appearing on the Golf Channel's *American Triumvirate*, recalled playing with Ben one day. While they both watched another player hit a shot, Ben turned to Jackie after the ball was away and asked, "Did you see that?" Jackie asked Ben what he was talking about. "He only waggled twice. He's been waggling three times up to now." Jackie added, "That's why Ben Hogan was called the Hawk. He saw everything—the grip, the balance of one's swing, the nervousness of his opponent—and this way he always seemed to have an advantage."

The 1948 US Open was the landmark point when the patrons of Los Angeles started to refer to Riviera as Hogan's Alley. Ben won another major later in the year—the PGA Championship, for the second time. He went on to win nine other regular tour events. He won the Vardon Trophy for the third time, and was at the top of the money list for the fourth time. Just when it looked like nothing was going to stop the Hawk, the fateful year of 1949 rolled around.

Left to right, front row: Bobby Jones, Ben Hogan.
Back row: Jimmy Demaret, Byron Nelson.
AP Wire Photo.

9

NEAR-FATAL ACCIDENT

JACQUE: *The Hogan family was excited about the prospects for 1949. Uncle Ben had been very successful in '47 and '48, and he was playing well. My father Royal had won the men's club championship at Colonial in 1948, following his first club win in 1944. We all felt that even better things were yet to come. I was in my first year of high school, and everything seemed to be coming up roses.*

Ben won the Bing Crosby Invitational to start 1949 off right, and then he defeated good friend and four-ball partner, Jimmy Demaret, in a playoff to win the Long Beach Open. Before regular commercial air travel became routine, and when trains were not convenient to take on a particular cir-

cuit, the tour players in the late 1940s would caravan or carpool from one tournament to another. The Demaret and Hogan caravan's next stop was Phoenix, where they tied again, forcing a playoff between the two fellow Texans for the second tournament in a row. This time Demaret would come out with a rare victory over his friend. The two were having drinks after the playoff, and Jimmy told Ben he was looking forward to a rubber match in Tucson, the tour's next stop. But Ben told Jimmy that he and Valerie were going to return to Fort Worth. He explained they had purchased a new house only a week before the tour started. "No sense having a house if we don't live in it," Ben said.

He told Jimmy that they wanted to get

back to Fort Worth so Valerie could start decorating the interior of their new home with recently purchased furniture. Ben and Valerie bid farewell to the Demarets, and as they were leaving, Ben told them he would see them in San Antonio at the Texas Open. Ben drove nine hours to El Paso on the first day of February, and then chose to drive on to Van Horn, about 120 miles east of El Paso. He hoped this would make the next day's drive to Fort Worth a little easier.

JACQUE: *Another thing my father and Uncle Ben had in common was that they both did all of the driving on trips. They very rarely wanted to stop. If my mother or I wanted a restroom stop or maybe a soda, it practically took an act of Congress to get Daddy to pull over.*

ROBERT: *On the road Ben and Valerie talked a lot, mostly about their new home on Valley Ridge Road in Fort Worth. They discussed the new furniture Valerie had purchased, and how she would arrange it in the two-story house. They also talked about the marital problems that Valerie's younger sister Sarah was having with her husband Walter. Divorce seemed inevitable and this bothered Valerie, probably because [it projected] the image of failure. Even though Valerie disliked having houseguests, she suggested that it might be good for Sarah and her five-year-old daughter Valerie to move in with them until the situation was resolved.*

Ben Hogan, always sharply dressed, comes down the stairs behind the old Colonial clubhouse.
JHT family collection.

Arriving in Van Horn, Ben drove directly to the Hotel El Capitan, where he had stayed on several occasions before. This was a favorite stopping place for touring pros because the rooms were clean and not expensive, and the home-cooked food was good. Ben could get his regular breakfast of scrambled eggs, crisp bacon, toast, and coffee at any time of the day, and he did that at about 6:30 on the morning of February 2nd. The next day was his father's birthday, a date fatefully burned into Ben's mind, along with February 22nd, the day his father died. Chester was thirty-seven when he fatally shot himself, and Ben would be thirty-seven the following August. This was weighing a little on Ben's mind as he finished his breakfast.

Ben and Valerie left the hotel about 8:00 a.m., and they headed east on Highway 80 toward Fort Worth, a drive of another eight or nine hours. A heavy fog had rolled in and limited visibility to several hundred feet. Ben was a conservative driver, and very cautious in bad weather. He rarely reached thirty miles per hour in the thick fog. But coming west on Highway 80 was a Greyhound bus traveling at approximately fifty miles per hour. The bus driver soon moved up behind a slow-running freight hauler, and being behind schedule, he made the fateful decision to pass the truck in the fog on what he thought was a long rise in the road. The Hogans' Cadillac was slowly coming up a slight rise in the highway. The thick fog had intensified, and Ben could hardly see past the front of the car. For what must have been one terrifying instant, Ben and Valerie stared at the bright headlights in front of them.

JACQUE: *At the last second Uncle Ben saw the bus was going to hit his side of the car, so he instinctively dove to his right. It has been written that he threw himself across Valerie's lap in an attempt to save her from the impact of the collision, but I'm not sure he had any time to think about it. Uncle Ben later told me he was only trying to get out of harm's way.*

The move probably saved both of their lives, because the massive crash drove the steering column back through the driver's seat and hurled the engine into the front passenger's seat. Ben's body took the brunt of the impact, and Valerie was hardly injured.

Several people stopped to help, but they each thought someone else had already called for an ambulance. One person thought that Ben was dead, while Valerie insisted that he was still alive. About an hour and a half later, paramedics arrived and confirmed that Ben had a pulse. They took him to Van Horn for x-rays and then on to the Hotel Dieu Hospital in El Paso, a facility managed by the Sisters of Charity of the Catholic Church. It took four long hours before Ben arrived at the El Paso hospital. The collision with the bus fractured his left collarbone, his pelvis, his left ankle, and several ribs. The doctors' original prognosis at Hotel Dieu gave him a very slim chance of survival.

JACQUE: *I do not remember who called us at home to tell us about the accident—perhaps it was Valerie or someone from the media. Mother called my school and left a message that Uncle Ben had been in a bad*

The Hogans' Cadillac, totaled in the accident near Van Horn.
After it was towed to Fort Worth in the spring of 1949, the
wrecked automobile was displayed on Leonard's lot downtown for two weeks or more.
Courtesy of Colonial Country Club, Fort Worth, Texas.

car accident. I was to come home as soon as possible, but I was to drive very carefully. My father had recently bought me a beautiful green 1949 Ford convertible, so I could get to and from school. My daddy and Valerie's sister Sarah flew to El Paso that afternoon, saw Ben, and talked to several of the doctors. After a couple of days, Daddy called home to tell us that Ben's condition was not as serious as first thought.

Royal was relieved that his younger brother would be all right, even though he knew his body was severely damaged. Ben was encased in a cast from his knees to his chest, and he had another cast on his fractured ankle. Friends and family were immensely relieved to hear the news, because until then most thought Ben would die. At the time, nobody had even considered whether Ben would ever play golf again, but Royal was convinced that he would not only walk again, but play golf again, too. The doctors were not so optimistic. Ben's condition improved quickly, however, and after a couple of weeks, the doctors predicted it might be only a few more days before Ben was able to return to Fort Worth. Then on February 18, a day before Ben was to leave, he suddenly felt a sharp pain in this chest. X-rays revealed a blood clot nearing his heart and two more moving from his left leg to his chest. He was given a blood thinner and told to stay at rest. A week later another

clot appeared in his leg and began moving toward his heart.

Dr. Howard Ditto, Ben's brother-in-law and a general surgeon in Fort Worth, flew to El Paso to visit Ben and was appalled by the casts. He took Royal out into the hallway and told him they had to get the casts off immediately, or Ben would continue to clot and have circulation issues. He felt Ben's condition would require the services of a surgical specialist to operate, or Ben would not survive much longer. Dr. Ditto suggested contacting Dr. Alton S. Ochsner, a professor at Tulane University Medical School and considered by many to be the best vascular surgeon in the country. Royal called Dr. Ochsner, who agreed to perform an extremely delicate procedure to tie off the primary vein that returns blood from the extremities of the body back to the heart and lungs. It was explained to Valerie and Royal that a successful operation could make walking very difficult for Ben, perhaps impossible. That was not the news they wanted to hear, but at least Ben might survive. Although Dr. Ochsner had agreed to come immediately to El Paso, a tropical storm and heavy rain had temporarily grounded all commercial flights leaving New Orleans. An effort to secure a charter flight was not successful, and Royal knew something had to be arranged to get Dr. Ochsner to El Paso.

Marty Leonard recalled, "I remember being awakened by the telephone in the middle of the night. Mr. Hogan, Royal that is, had called my dad to seek his advice on how to get a doctor from New Orleans to El Paso. My dad was very, very upset about Ben's condition."

Marvin and Royal discussed options, and it was decided Royal would seek the help of Ben's old Tarrant Field commander and exhibition golf partner, David Hutchinson, now a brigadier general. Royal hung up, promptly called the air force base, and asked to speak with General Hutchinson about a matter of life and death. The general listened to Royal describe Ben's plight. When Hutchinson hung up he issued a command that would send a B-29 bomber from Carswell Air Force Base to New Orleans to pick up Dr. Ochsner.. Eight hours later, a B-29 landed at Biggs Air Force Base in El Paso, and Dr. Ochsner was rushed to Ben's bedside at the Hotel Dieu Hospital. Dr. Ochsner advised surgery—immediately. Valerie wouldn't agree to the operation, however, unless Ben approved. After Ben regained consciousness, the doctor explained the procedure.

Ben responded, "Are you going to fix me so that I can play golf again?"

It was Dr. Ochsner's opinion that Ben would be lucky if he ever walked properly again, much less play golf, but he did not share his true thoughts with the Hogans.

He only offered that if the operation didn't proceed soon, Ben would most likely die. Ben agreed to leave it in the good doctor's hands and approved the procedure. After they wheeled Ben away, Valerie went to the hospital chapel to pray for the duration of her husband's two-hour operation.

The next day's headline in the *El Paso Times* read: "Ben Hogan Out of Danger After Surgery." The Friday, March 4, 1949, article, reported by Scott Thurber, stated in part:

> Bantam Ben Hogan was "out of danger" and back on the road to recovery Thursday night in Hotel Dieu, following an operation necessitated by a serious blood clot condition. Dr. Alton Ochsner, surgical specialist who flew in from New Orleans Thursday afternoon, said the operation was a "complete success" and predicted a complete recovery for the diminutive golf champion.
>
> "He should recover from the effects of surgery within a week and be up and around in a few months," the surgeon said.
>
> Hogan had been reported in serious condition most of the day Thursday. Dr. Ochsner, professor of surgery at Tulane University and head of the Ochsner Clinic in New Orleans, said a large clot had appeared

late Wednesday night. A smaller clot had been discovered several days previous. The doctor said he had made an incision in the golfer's abdomen and tied off the vein through which the clots had appeared.

"It was similar to turning off a water faucet," Dr. Ochsner said. "We removed the danger of any more clots—and another one could have been fatal."

The two clots, which had endangered the golf star's life, had been absorbed by his system, according to the surgeon. Following the operation Thursday night, his wife, Valerie, and his brother, Royal Hogan of Fort Worth, expressed confidence that Bantam Ben had nothing but time remaining between him and complete recovery. Royal Hogan would make no predictions concerning his brother's release from the hospital.

"But the danger is over," he said, "and we're all happy about that."

Dr. Ochsner said the little golfing ace apparently had been in critical condition for a time following the appearance of the second clot Wednesday night. Hogan was given "a large transfusion" before submitting to surgery. The eminent New Orleans surgeon, who flew here in an army plane, was to leave El Paso at 12:45 a.m. on a chartered ship for his return home.

As the article described, the lengthy operation by Dr. Ochsner was a success. Ben survived, but his left shoulder and both legs would hurt every day for the rest of his life.

JACQUE: *When Daddy called us with the news, we were delighted and, I might add, a few prayers were offered. None of us cared whether Uncle Ben ever played golf again. Fans from around the world responded to the news of his near-fatal accident with flowers, letters, and telegrams, which overflowed his hospital room. He had literally shut fans out of his thoughts while he was playing golf, and now he experienced an overwhelming feeling of humility for the outpouring of care and support from people he didn't know. There's no doubt in my mind that this revelation provided the motivation for him to get back on his feet and play golf again. But it also put further responsibility on him–a greater sense of obligation he felt to all those people cheering him on. I believed that if and when Uncle Ben played golf again, it would be for the fans.*

Slowly, Ben's condition improved, but he still faced surgery on his shoulder and perhaps one of his knees. The doctors were not as optimistic about a full recovery, but Ben was determined. No one except Ben, Valerie, and

In a photo discovered by Bill Wood, John Payne, Mary Beth Hughes, Ben Hogan and George "Gabby" Hayes joke around during Ben's recovery at the Hotel Dieu Hospital in El Paso. The actors visited Ben to cheer him up while they were in town for the premiere of their movie *El Paso*.
AP Wire Photo.

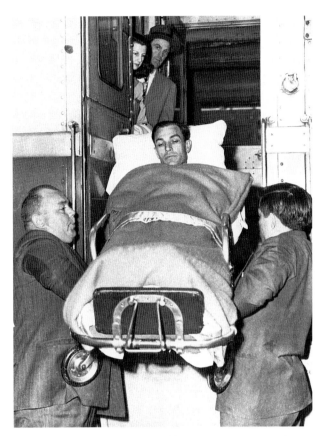

Ben Hogan being lifted down off the train in Fort Worth after his stay in the El Paso hospital. In the background, a concerned Valerie and Royal Hogan look on.
Copyright Bettman/Corbis / AP Images.

Royal thought Ben would ever play competitive golf again.

Ben's recovery was a step-by-step process. He increased his activities slowly, but with certainty. He committed himself to doing something every day to get better, even while still in bed. He would stretch his hands, opening and closing them over and over, clutching them like he was holding a golf club. He relentlessly squeezed a small rubber ball to strengthen his hands and forearms. When he progressed to sitting on the edge of the bed, he flexed his dangling legs and concentrated on exercising the muscles he used in a golf swing.

Ben left the Hotel Dieu Hospital on April 1, 1949, and he and Valerie returned to Fort Worth by train. Royal flew out to make the trip back with them. Family members and many friends were on hand to welcome Ben home at the Texas & Pacific Railway terminal in downtown Fort Worth.

JACQUE: *What I remember most about seeing Uncle Ben lowered from the train in a stretcher was how thin and drawn he looked. His appearance was a lot worse than I had expected. But he was happy to be home and truly lucky to be alive.*

10

"HIS LEGS WEREN'T STRONG ENOUGH TO CARRY HIS HEART"

Ben had spent two months in the Hotel Dieu Hospital—a significant part of that time in what amounted to a full body cast. Nobody but his wife, his brother, and Marvin Leonard believed he had the slightest chance of returning to the tour or, for that matter, of playing golf at all.

JACQUE: *I was horrified to see how bad Uncle Ben looked. He had lost a lot of weight. I went to his house to see him every chance I got. He pushed himself daily, walking first around the house, then the yard, then down the street. There were times when Valerie had to pick him up in the car because he had pushed himself to the limit and couldn't make it back to the house.*

People had heard the reports and read about the seriousness of his surgeries. They had seen photos of the wrecked car, the body cast, and the gaunt physique, but what they couldn't see was the intensity of Ben's pride, the girth of his determination, or the size of his heart. Ben's attempt to recover proved to be the most difficult task in his life, but he looked at his rehabilitation like a round of golf—one shot at a time, leading to one hole at a time, until the round is finished. Ben knew he had to get the strength back in his legs, but his broken ribs and fractured pelvis were healing slowly. It was going to be a painful process to get to the point where he could walk eighteen holes.

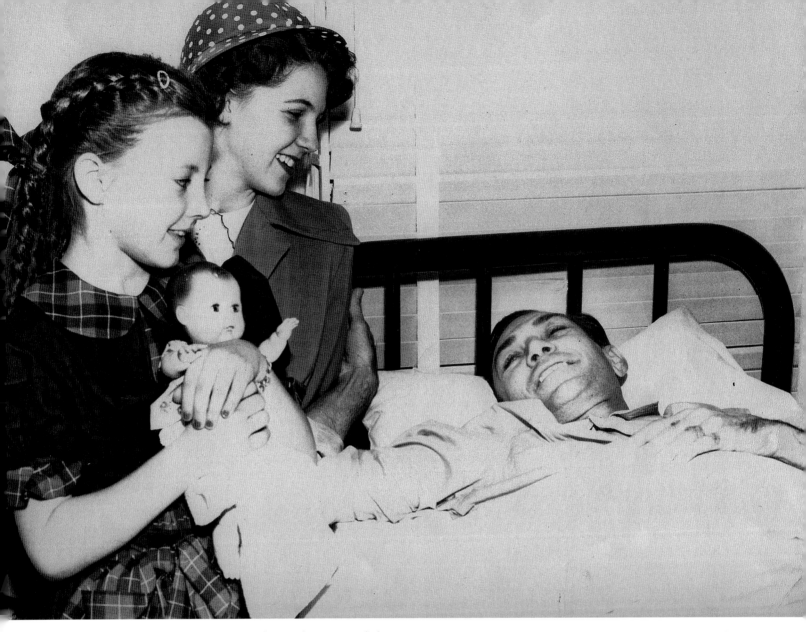

Ben's nieces Valerie Harriman and Jacqueline Hogan glad
to see their uncle home and doing better.
AP Wire Photo.

JACQUE: *Uncle Ben had developed phlebitis, so to prevent any further blood clots, for the rest of his life he had to wear support stockings up to his thighs to aid the circulation. He was in a lot of pain, but amazingly he worked through it. Valerie had some help with Uncle Ben at their new home on Valley Ridge, as Sarah had accepted her sister's invitation to live with them. There was an extra bedroom upstairs, which Sarah and her daughter moved into. Uncle Ben liked Sarah's company because she was the life of the party and made him laugh. Valerie was noticeably happier and more relaxed when Sarah was around. Sarah was good at the details of domestic life—cooking, washing dishes and clothes, and general housework, which Valerie appreciated, especially with Ben in his present condition.*

Ben started his path to rehabilitation with small walks around the living room using a walker, until he traded it for a cane, which was actually a putter with a rubber tip on the end of the grip. Then he started to wear out the carpet taking small steps, perhaps only ten at first, then fifteen, then twenty, until he was ready to try the outdoors. The first venture out, Ben attempted to walk around the house, but he would have to stop a few times before he finished. After another week, he was attempting to walk around the block. At first, he only walked part way down the street. He walked until he had to sit down on the curb, where he would wait for Valerie to come pick him up. He eventually made it around the block, then pushed on until he could walk the block two times. At one point, he managed to mix in some light running.

His good friend on the tour, Jimmy Demaret, was amazed at the Hawk's optimism, especially when Ben sat down one day in May, only a short six weeks after his release from the hospital, and wrote a letter to the USGA. He surprised the headquarters with a short letter describing his hope to enter the 1949 US Open in June. He asked the organization not to release his desire to the press, for he wished it to be a surprise. But, of course, he was being a little too optimistic. Ben felt he had to set goals to push himself for further recovery.

On May 17th, overnight, eleven inches of rain fell upstream on the Clear Fork of the Trinity and its watershed, as the river entered the western edge of Fort Worth. The intensity of the rain over such a short period of time overflowed the levees and flooded a great deal of the city's northwestern development. The flood was the worst in Fort Worth's history, causing $11 million in damage, destroying over a thousand buildings, killing eleven citizens, and leaving thirteen thousand people homeless.

JACQUE: *The rains and flooding happened*

at night, so everybody was home asleep. Daddy tried to drive to his store, but the flooding blocked his usual way to downtown. He came by the house and told us about the rising water at Colonial. He turned to me and said, "Do not get in your car and go down there. Hear me! Don't go down there." "No, Daddy, I wouldn't think of going down there. Not me." I let him get out of sight and jumped in my car immediately. I drove down to the club, and when I got there Daddy appeared out of nowhere and scolded me. He always caught me when I did anything he had forbidden me to do. He had to find a different way to get to his store, and eventually went all the way around the southern part of Fort Worth to get downtown. What I saw at Colonial was terrible—only the clubhouse was above water, and it was threatened. The entire golf course was covered by several feet of floodwater.

A fireman had to pilot a boat to rescue Colonial greens superintendent Joe Cano and his family from the roof of their two-story stone home, situated adjacent to the course.

A longtime Colonial member, Don Matheson, remembered, "We drove over to Colonial and the water was over the street past the pool. Everything was under water other than the clubhouse. Milton Lamoy, one of the greensmen, lived with his father in the caddyshack. They were washed out of bed during the night by the rushing waters, and we saw them both in a tree on the second fairway holding on for dear life. They stayed there all morning before they were finally rescued."

The next day, James Cotton of the US Army Corps of Engineers reported, "It was primarily a flood of the Clear Fork that was swelled by heavy rainfalls on the lower Clear Fork and the lower part of its watershed. It was simply too much water for the levees."

The Montgomery Ward building's entire first floor was submerged in the rising waters, and nearby at "Six Points"—the corner of West Seventh Street, Camp Bowie Boulevard, University Drive, and Bailey Avenue—resembled a small lake. This was an entire mile north of the banks of the Trinity. The waterworks downtown were completely submerged, disabling the motors that pumped the city's water to its citizens. The Fort Worth City Council asked all nonessential businesses without a private water supply to close until the situation improved. A new motor had to be brought by truck from Indianapolis. In Oklahoma, the truck driver bringing the motor was pulled over for speeding, and when the state trooper learned what the truck was carrying, he informed the driver every patrol from Missouri to Texas was looking for him to aid in getting the essential shipment to Fort Worth. The patrolman along with other officers escorted the truck to Fort Worth, where the new motor was delivered only thirty-three hours after it left Indiana.

Floodwaters from Fort Worth's major 1949 flood cover the entire golf course at Colonial. The clubhouse, located on the highest ground, was spared damage.
Courtesy of Colonial Country Club, Fort Worth, Texas.

Nine days later, after additional rainfall, eight greens at Colonial were still underwater, so on May 26th the upcoming fourth annual Colonial National Invitational was cancelled. Even though River Crest Country Club, which had escaped the flooding, offered their course for the tournament, the tournament committee declined their offer.

Marvin Leonard sent a statement to the newspapers: *We're canceling the tournament because the city has been struck by tragedy, and we feel that this is no time to hold a golf tournament. The club and our members will best serve the needs of the community by getting involved in relief efforts.*

Marvin and his brother Obie had already been helping in all the ways they could. The day after the heavy rains, as the floodwaters continued to rise, the two brothers leaped into action. They outfitted their store personnel with boats and outboard motors from the sporting goods department and sent them out to rescue folks in flooded neighborhoods west of Leonard's. As the floodwaters receded, the Leonard brothers' employees returned to their ruined homes and picked up appliances disabled by the waters such as stoves, washers, refrigerators, and even pianos. They brought them to the store for free repairs. The Leonard brothers proved to be saviors at a time of real tragedy.

It took weeks for all of the standing water to recede, so it was good that Marvin and his committee had cancelled the Colonial NIT. Besides, as some folks thought, what would a Colonial Invitational be if their favorite son, Ben Hogan, couldn't play? After all, in the first three NIT's, Ben had two victories and a tie for second.

Near the end of summer, as Fort Worth was beginning to mend, Ben was also working hard on completing his recovery. He silently vowed to himself that he would not miss the US Open in 1950.

Ben showed up at Colonial one day in August of 1949 and headed for the practice range to hit balls. It took him months, hitting as many balls as his body allowed, before he started to approach his old distances, especially with the driver. Ben eventually became resigned to the fact he might never recover the pre-accident distances with his drives, so he spent hours practicing with his one, two, and three irons, so he would be prepared for longer approaches to the greens.

JACQUE: *Uncle Ben had started planning a trip to California in January to play in the Los Angeles Open at the Riviera Country Club, one of his favorite courses. After practicing for several months, his first round of golf was with my daddy the day after Christmas in 1949. He had to use a golf cart that first round, but soon he was able to walk the course, and he felt he was ready for Los Angeles.*

Ben was determined to play again, and he felt there was no better place to make the attempt than at Riviera, where he had won several times. Ben practiced even more than usual for his comeback entry to the professional tour. When he arrived at Riviera only eleven months after the accident, Jimmy Demaret, a frequent partner with Ben during practice rounds, commented that Ben had calluses on his hands from hitting so many practice shots in preparation for the tournament. Of course calluses were not new to Ben. He once told a golfer who had complained of blisters beneath his calluses that one needed to work the calluses all the way to the bone. He impressed Demaret and his playing partners when he finished his first practice round at Riviera with a 68. They felt he was back, and maybe even the man to beat. They probably didn't know that Ben was so tired and in such pain that he collapsed on his bed when he returned to his hotel room. While soaking his legs in Epsom salts, he actually began to doubt whether he could play a seventy-two-hole tournament with thirty-six holes on the last day, but he was determined to give it a try.

The fans at Riviera received Ben Hogan like they never had before. Jimmy Demaret later wrote, "Ben had requested the announcer, Scotty Chisholm, to introduce him simply. Scotty, in his kilts and tam, followed Ben's wishes almost, saying, 'This is the greatest event in the history of the Los Angeles Open. But, I have been requested by Mr. Hogan to introduce him and say nothing else. On the tee is Ben Hogan!' The gallery's response could only be described as a roar."

Ben was taken aback by the response and the enthusiastic reception. He backed off his tee shot, and as the gallery continued to applaud he actually bowed his head a little, acknowledging the well-wishers. His response was a respectable first round of 73, very much in contention. That night he soaked his aching legs in Epsom salts and massaged them to increase the circulation and prevent swelling. This would become a familiar routine for the rest of Ben's life. He believed his legs were the critical factor in his continuing tournament play, although many believed that it was his heart. Any comeback would require both.

Ben then registered three straight rounds of 69, some of which were played in the rain. Following his last putt on the seventy-second hole, he waited in the clubhouse for Sam Snead to finish his fourth round. Sam was the only remaining player to have a chance of winning, or at least tying Ben, for the leading seventy-two-hole score. Snead sank a forty-foot putt for a birdie on the eighteenth hole, for an excellent final round of 66, forcing an eighteen-hole playoff to be scheduled the next day. The rain continued, however,

Royal (left) and Ben (right) tee off at Colonial.
Photos probably taken at the 1950 NIT Pro-Am.
JHT family collection.

and a conflict in Snead's schedule delayed the playoff for a week. When they finally got it in, Ben did not play well, and Sam won the tournament.

The night after the playoff, two sportswriters hosted a dinner at Riviera to honor Ben. The iconic journalist Grantland Rice made a speech that is famous in sports lore. During his remarks, Rice said, "We have gathered here tonight to honor a man who record books will show lost a tournament today. I say he didn't lose. His legs simply were not strong enough to carry his heart around."

Ben returned to Fort Worth and got a few days of rest before he became a regular sight on the Colonial practice range once again. Two months later, he was at Augusta National attempting to win his first Masters. In that tournament Ben finished a respectable fourth and lost to his good friend Jimmy Demaret by seven strokes. Ben wasn't satisfied until three weeks later when he dominated the tournament at Greenbrier, shooting a 259 on Sam Snead's home course in the Allegheny Mountains at Sulphur Springs, West Virginia. This was the lowest total for a seventy-two-hole score in a PGA event.

Marty Leonard remarked, "For an athlete that's had an injury as serious as Ben experienced, and to come back and play through the anguish and pain and play at such a high level—it was quite amazing to see. We all knew what he had to go through with his legs, wrapping them all of the time, the nightly treatments, the occasional rubdowns. We all knew he was in pain when he was walking those fairways. What he accomplished is one of the most courageous stories of determination, bull-headedness, and ultimate comebacks in the annals of sport."

After the Greenbrier, Ben returned to Fort Worth, where he finished third at the 1950 Colonial NIT, and he was met again with a roar of admiration from the galleries. The Hawk, a golfer many had thought to be arrogant or standoffish when he played in tournaments before the accident, was now looked on as an inspirational sportsman. He was held in the highest esteem by fellow golfers as well as throngs of new fans.

Several innovations were introduced at the 1950 Colonial tournament. Fort Worth station WBAP-TV broadcast the weekend rounds to homes in the area—the first tour event other than the 1947 US Open (when station KSD-TV had broadcast to the St. Louis area) to televise locally for the benefit of fans unable to attend. The local broadcast would continue every year until 1964, when ABC began to televise the Colonial Invitational to the entire nation. Also making its debut in 1950 was the five-foot-tall J. Marvin Leonard trophy presented to the winner. The trophy had been created for the 1949 event, but because the flood had forced the cancellation of the tournament, 1950 would be the first year it was awarded. Marvin Leonard presented his namesake trophy to the winner, Sam Snead.

ROBERT: *On May 13, 1950, just fifteen months after the accident, Ben played in an exhibition match at Lions Municipal Golf Course in Austin, Texas. In April of 2010, a friend called to tell Jacque and me about a charity event in which her uncle would be honored, and we jumped at the opportunity to attend. We weren't aware that Ben had played golf in Austin and were excited that he was to be recognized. The event was held to raise money to save "Old Muny" from being developed by the landowner, the University of Texas.*

At the event called "The Legends of Lions," each of the holes was named after golfers who had played Old Muny. They were voted on by fans all over Texas. Hole number sixteen was named after Ben Hogan. This was a very enjoyable and touching experience for us, because I played golf at Old Muny for a number of years when I lived in Austin. One of my dearest friends and a dedicated admirer of Ben Hogan, Austin's Ben Crenshaw, was also there to accept the honor of having hole number one named for him.

Jacque thought it was in Ben's heart to give something back to the fans when he decided to play that 1950 match in Austin. His partner was Harvey Penick, the legendary coach and author of the Little Red Book, *and their opposing team consisted of two outstanding University of Texas golfers—Morris Williams Jr. and Ed Hopkins. When they played the sixteenth hole, Ben hit his drive near trees on the right side of the fairway. A good drive ended up in a valley, and one could not see the results of a drive from the tee box due to a mound in front of the tee. When Ben reached his ball he was heard to exclaim, "This is the only hole I've ever seen without a fairway." Remarkably, he hit a five iron off the rocks through the trees and over the water, landing in front of the green and rolling up to five feet from the pin. Ben birdied the hole, and it's been known as the "Hogan Hole" ever since, made official on that inspirational April day back in 2010.*

The story goes that in the Austin exhibition match, Ben gave the gallery and his partner, Harvey Penick, something to remember. He showed a side of himself that few if any had ever seen. He showed up late for the scheduled tee time, staggered onto the first tee box with his famous white golf cap on sideways. He swung at the ball and whiffed it. Spectators were appalled to see the world-renowned Ben Hogan address the ball, waggle a couple of times and swing again, this time knocking the ball backwards off the tee box. His caddy replaced the ball on a yellow wooden tee, and Ben topped his drive about fifty yards down the fairway. One can only imagine the crowd was stunned.

Ben's next shot was a big slice, and in the process of swinging at the ball his cap fell off. Finally on the green he putted past the hole by about twenty feet, and then putted back, again about twenty feet past the cup. Staggering like he was drunk, he lined up his putt with a plumb-bob effort and sunk it for a seven. He then fell down retrieving his ball from the cup.

This was Hogan "the Clown," revealing a sense of humor that was relatively unknown to sports writers and the general public. Ben looked around at the befuddled fans, smiled, and said to Mr. Penick, "Okay pardner, it's up to you on this hole. I'll do better from now on." Ben finished with a round of 67 on his own ball, and he and Mr. Penick won the match two up.

Both Ben and Byron Nelson, who had also played Austin's Old Muny at one time, had been quoted as praising this course as one of the finest public golf courses in the country. For Ben's sake, and the golfers of Texas who have enjoyed playing Lions Municipal, Jacque and I both hope they save Old Muny from the developer's bulldozers.

Ben Hogan clowning around on the first tee at Austin's Lions Municipal Golf Course while playing in an exhibition with Harvey Penick. JHT family collection.

The next tournament for Ben in his comeback was the US Open at Merion Golf Club, outside of Philadelphia, the event he marked on his calendar the previous year before he was able to swing a golf club. The 1950 Open would be played on Merion's East Course, famous site of Bobby Jones's victory in the

1930 US Amateur, where the great Georgian completed the only "Grand Slam" in golf history. Over the par 70 layout, Ben had first rounds of 72, 69, and 72, and would start the final round two strokes behind fellow Texan Lloyd Mangrum. In those days the final day of a tournament consisted of thirty-six holes played on Saturday, and as he had done earlier in the year, Ben would walk up and down the rugged fairways, playing through the pain in both the morning and afternoon rounds, his legs wrapped from ankle to thigh. In the final round, Ben played the first eleven holes in one-over par and turned a two-stroke deficit to Mangrum into a two-stroke lead, and it looked as if he might run away with the tournament in the final eight holes. His putter failed him coming in, however, and he bogeyed numbers twelve, fifteen, and seventeen. He would require a par on the eighteenth hole to force a playoff with Mangrum and George Fazio, who had completed play with a seven over par 287. Hogan didn't drive the ball long on eighteen, but he was in the center of the fairway, which would lead to the iconic photograph of one of the most famous shots of his career—a one iron that delivered the ball to within forty feet of the pin. He calmly two-putted to force a three-way playoff to be contested on Sunday.

In the playoff, the three players were within one stroke of each other after twelve holes.

Fazio could only manage a bogey on four of the last five holes. He fell out of contention, while Ben led Mangrum by a single stroke through fifteen. As Mangrum prepared to putt on the sixteenth, he picked up his ball to remove a bug that had landed on it and was assessed a two-stroke penalty, resulting in a double bogey. Ben would then birdie the seventeenth, the hole that had taken away his victory the day before, and he cruised to a four-stroke victory with his one-under 69.

This Open victory would be dubbed, "The Miracle at Merion," giving Ben his second "official" national championship. For the year 1950, Sam Snead won eleven tournaments and the Vardon Trophy with a stroke average of 69.23, a record that would stand for fifty years. In spite of Snead's incredible year, Ben Hogan earned his second Player of the Year award because of his courageous comeback from injury and adversity.

FACING PAGE: The most famous photograph in golf—the only picture Hy Peskin took during an entire day of following Ben Hogan. JHT family collection.

Ben Hogan

Ben advertises a beer.
JHT family collection.

In 1951, Ben entered only five PGA tour events, winning three that included a couple of majors, and he finished second and fourth in the other two tournaments. At the 1951 Masters, Ben finally earned his first green jacket; coming from one shot back, he shot a masterful final round of 68 to win the tournament by two strokes. Actually, the green jacket that had been worn by members since 1937 was not presented to the tournament winner until 1952, but it was considered retroactive for previous winners as a denotation for a Masters Champion.

At the US Open, held June 14th–16th at Oakland Hills Country Club in Birmingham, Michigan, northwest of Detroit, Ben would shoot a final round 67, one of only two rounds under par for the entire tournament. He finished seven over par, coming from two shots back after fifty-four holes to win by two strokes. Not counting 1949, when Ben couldn't compete, this would be the third straight national championship for the Hawk. Except for missing the US Open in 1949 and again in 1957 due to injury, from 1940 to 1960 Ben won four times and never finished out of the top ten.

In 1951, Ben won the World Championship of Golf at the Tam O'Shanter Country Club in the Chicago suburb of Niles, Illinois. The tournament had the largest purse to that date, with $10,000 awarded the winner. Ex-

The brothers Hogan.
JHT family collection.

cept for the US Open, which had increased to $4,000, a normal winner's total at this time very rarely exceeded $2,000.

The 1951 Colonial would draw the most attention to Ben, but his new high-profile celebrity status probably had less to do with the tournament than it did with *Follow the Sun*, a new biographical movie based on Ben Hogan's life. The movie debuted at three Fort Worth theaters and was the talk of the town.

All the fuss it created made Ben's victory at Colonial even more prominent and newsworthy, leading some of his fellow professional golfers to jokingly refer to the 1951 Colonial NIT as the Ben Hogan Benefit Tournament.

JACQUE: *The surge in fan support for Uncle Ben in 1950 was followed by an interest in Hollywood for the story of his life. The subsequent movie, entitled* Follow the Sun, *was advertised as the story of Ben Hogan's life, but it turned out to be a fairly poor representation of his golf life, the accident, and his recovery. For me, and most of our family, the movie was a terrible disappointment. First, it was difficult to picture Glenn Ford as Ben Hogan. Ford, a very good actor, was not a golfer, and he never learned to swing a golf club with any serious credibility. I felt his efforts would never convince viewers that he was who he was supposed to be. I could not accept the premise that I was watching a part of history, since I knew Uncle Ben's life story. The movie was merely a caricature with too much fluff added for effect, and fictional characters made up to provide dramatic sequences that never happened. More important to me was the total absence of a character portraying Mama Hogan. She was a very strong woman, dedicated to her children, and she had more influence on Uncle Ben, Daddy and their sister Princess than any other person in their lives. She was too important a member of the Hogan family to leave out. It was Hollywood after all, and like so many of its supposedly true stories, the truth was lost in the movie's portrayal of the "facts." One thing the movie did accomplish, however, was that it added to the fan support for Uncle Ben, for which I am grateful.*

Ben would end his shortened 1951 golf experience playing on the US Ryder Cup team, captained by Sam Snead, at Pinehurst, North Carolina, November 2–4. Ben teamed with his old partner and fellow Texan Jimmy Demaret to win the Friday foursomes match five and four, over the British team of Fred Daly and Ken Bousfield. During the Sunday singles competition, Ben beat Charlie Ward three and two.

A remarkable year, 1951 ended with the PGA of America voting Ben Player of the Year for the third time in the four years the award had been in existence. His comeback was complete and stunning. But unbeknownst to anyone, the best year of his professional golf career was still ahead of him.

11

"IF USED IN AN OFFICE, WE HAVE IT!"

In 1943, Royal Hogan celebrated the eighth anniversary of his Fort Worth Office Supply Company with his store's most profitable year. His young company had survived the Depression and had grown every year of its existence. Part of Royal Hogan's success lay in his careful control of every aspect of his business—a tendency to control that actually extended to every part of his life. Superb customer service and Royal's strategic alliances with the fine manufacturers of office furniture were also key factors in his success, and by the mid-1940s the company had become one of the fastest-growing businesses in Texas.

One of the early suppliers was General Fireproofing, famous for developing the first four-drawer fireproofed metal file cabinet and the first fireproof safe. Fort Worth Office Supply became the agent for this Youngstown, Ohio, furniture manufacturer during the 1930s, and Royal continued that association into the 1970s. Many of Royal's clients stocked their offices with the General Fireproofing line of steel desks and chairs, file cabinets, and other office items. But GF, as the furniture company was known in the industry, was only one of many suppliers Royal's company had contracted to represent.

Most of Fort Worth's major business concerns, including Texaco Oil, Gulf Oil, and the larger Fort Worth banks, loved the lines of top-rated products that Fort Worth Office

Front view of Royal Hogan's office supply company at
1007 Main Street, Fort Worth.
JHT family collection.

Supply provided. Royal didn't ignore the little operators or the general public, however, and provided more modestly priced products for their businesses and homes.

Royal had several loyal employees and salesmen who stayed with him for many years—people like Elmo Dungan and H. E. Nesmith, two experienced salesmen who were with the company from the 1930s into the 1950s. Later, Glenn Little served as store manager, and Jack Clemons was office manager. Both were hard-working men who brought a lot to the company and served Royal Hogan for many loyal years, as did another salesman, Arch Boulware, who served as the purchasing agent. These were all people that Royal trusted to keep the company on track and operating his way when he was following his brother on the golf circuit or playing in an amateur event himself. All of the salesmen worked the floor, but some worked in the field or the "streets."

As Royal was quoted in a *Fort Worth Press* article, "If a customer is unable to drop in and look over our lines personally we welcome all inquiries by telephone, and our salesmen will be glad to contact the customer and come meet with them at their convenience."

"Mr. Hogan was a very good salesman," declared Don Bassham, one of Royal's salesmen. "He could be very persuasive. If he signed with an insurance company, he made

Interior view of Main Street store showing the various office supplies available.
JHT family collection.

sure that company was a customer for the future. He would make small deposits in various banks, $5,000, sometimes only $1,000. And then he would have us call on the bank managers to get their business."

When Bassham came to work for Hogan's Fort Worth Office Supply in the 1950s, there were twelve employees. Among the employees there were three other salesmen, a delivery man/janitor, and a secretary, Mary Bedner, who was Royal's main bookkeeper and in charge of payroll.

JACQUE: *Daddy respected Mary and really depended on her. She was a very good secretary and served him loyally for decades before she retired.*

Royal Hogan on his way to call on a customer in downtown Fort Worth. He's wearing his summer boater purchased at Peters Brothers next door to Hogan Office Supply. JHT family collection.

Graydon E. Armstrong, an accountant, succeeded Mary to take control of the bookkeeping and payroll division. Royal had seen Mr. Armstrong working for a lumber business customer and thought he was a fine man, so he stole him away. In addition to Mr. Armstrong, there were two assistant bookkeepers working in the open space on a balcony overlooking the showroom. They each had a desk and assisted Mr. Armstrong and the sales force. The company also employed Mr. Dingler, who was originally hired to remodel a new building Royal purchased; he stayed on for years as the store's repairman.

JACQUE: *Everyone just called him Mr. Dingler. I never knew his first name. He could repair anything—desks, chairs, file cabinets—and then refinish them so they looked brand new.*

For awhile during the 1950s, Royal's father-in-law worked at the store. Jacque called her mother's parents, "BB" and "PawPaw".

JACQUE: *When BB and PawPaw's house on Jessamine was condemned to make way for the new Interstate, they closed down the sandwich factory. My grandfather went to work for Daddy in the office supply company at the Main Street location. Daddy put PawPaw in charge of all of the shipping and packing, as well as the incoming and outgoing deliveries. One day, and it isn't clear exactly how, PawPaw fell off of the elevator at the store and died. Apparently nobody witnessed the incident, they just found him dead. He had apparently hit his head in the fall and it killed him. That had a major effect on my dad. For many years, he felt responsible for his father-in-law's death.*

Don Bassham recalls, "When I first went to work for Fort Worth Office Supply, I was more or less a trainee, but Mr. Hogan put me on the street right away because I had had some experience in sales. He taught me his method of selling, and he gave me a stack of cards—people and businesses to call on—and I would call on them on a regular basis. Mr. Hogan had strong lines [of merchandise] with General Fireproofing, Stow & Davis Furniture, National Blank Book Company, Wallace Pencil Company, Dunlock Chairs, Herman Miller, Hoosier Desk Company, Carter's Ink Company, and many more."

The list of customers that Hogan's Fort Worth Office Supply served was a literal who's who of the top companies operating in Fort Worth, among them the Fort Worth National Bank, Union Bank, and Alcon Laboratories, and oil companies like Champlain, Texaco, and Gulf. Don Bassham and the other members of the sales force would make presentations to the customers they called on to demonstrate new lines. They would present everything they had to offer, take orders, and explain the delivery process. Howard Small ran the delivery system with great efficiency.

Howard Andrew Small, an African American, was born June 11, 1924, in Carthage, Texas. After serving his country honorably in the United States Navy, Howard, at the age of twenty-two, came to work for Fort Worth Office Supply as the shipping and receiving clerk. Howard would work for Royal for forty-

New City Golf Champ Is Business Man

FOR the first time in several years, the city golf champion is a business man golfer—one of the boys who tends to business all week and gets in a dollar-dollar-dollar game on Saturday afternoon and Sunday. Royal Hogan has been a member of Colonial for about six months. Ole Whalen, pro, says he doesn't remember seeing Hogan practice much if any. In fact, he hadn't even played for six weeks prior to the city tournament except about one week before qualifying day. Wilburn Davis, Press photographer, flashed the new champ as he sat at his desk at the Fort Worth Office Supply store which he conducts on Houston St. The elder brother of the now famous Ben Hogan seems tickled at knocking out three hot favorites in succession to achieve the title the hard way.

City champion Royal Hogan at his desk.
Photo by the *Fort Worth Press*.

three years at both Royal's store and at his home.

Don recalls, "Howard Small knew how to do everything. He was a complete handyman and jack-of-all-trades. He was very soft-spoken and very polite to my wife and children. He would help me a lot when I had to move from one location in town to another. Mr. Hogan would let us have the truck, and Howard would help us move. He was such an extremely generous man."

JACQUE: *Howard and Daddy had a wonderful, close relationship. And Howard helped raise my kids. He would be working*

THE FAMILY TRIBUTE

Howard Small sits at Royal Hogan's desk. This photograph was used for the tribute pamphlet at Howard's funeral. Courtesy of Don Bassham.

in the yard or around the house and he would hear one of my kids crying or something, and he could beat me to them. Howard was like a gentle giant. They weren't many people like him.

Howard Small was very loyal to all of the employees at Fort Worth Office Supply, and was always available to help out at the house of his boss, Royal, and his wife. Howard was also the overseer at the Fort Worth Office Supply store, keeping it tidy and aiding in the delivery. After a few years, Royal gave Howard the delivery truck to use to get to and from work. The truck was a flatbed with removable wooden side rails, which made it easy for furniture to be loaded or unloaded.

Don added, "He did it all. I never did think of Howard, as some people did in those days, as being black. I always thought of Howard Small as being a great part of our business. I always thought Mr. Hogan respected Howard a great deal, and didn't think about his race."

During the '50s and '60s, the elevators in most buildings were not large enough for some of the newer, bigger pieces of furniture. So Howard and other delivery men would place the furniture on top of the elevator, either at the store or at an office building they were remodeling. They strapped the furniture down, Howard would cautiously step on, hold onto the furniture, take it up to its destination, and unload it.

Don recalls, "You had to have the help and approval of the building managers to do this, but they would lower the elevator until its roof was at floor level, so the men could load and deliver the items to their appointed locations on any floor."

All of the employees contributed to the growth of the company, and Royal had the foresight to look ahead and plan a strategy.

Don recalls, "I approached Mr. Hogan a few times over the years about expanding the business, maybe incorporating, bringing in capital for growth. But he would have none of that talk."

JACQUE: *Daddy would have never incorporated, for he wouldn't have been in control. He had to be in control.*

Up to the 1960s all employees were paid a salary, and those who produced during the year would receive a bonus. Later on, as the business grew, Royal set a minimum, and if the sales exceeded a certain amount, the employees would receive a certain percentage as a commission. Fort Worth Office Supply had its own way of setting costs and pricing their products, and each new salesman was quickly introduced to Royal's unique coding system.

"This was the first time I had been in a business like this," Don Bassham revealed. "I had worked for Texas Electric and we had ledgers and did it a certain way. But Mr. Hogan's coding system was based on the word IMPORTANCE."

The *I* in *IMPORTANCE* stood for a 1, the *M* a 2, the *P* a 3, and so on to the *E* representing 0. When they got in merchandise, say a box of paper, and it cost the company a dollar, the coding machine would make a label to say I-00. If it were a twenty-five-dollar item, the code would read MR-00. In this way, the salesman always knew the cost of an item, and would make sure to have the proper markup when presenting the products to customers. It was a unique coding system, and one Royal was very proud of creating.

Don said, "Mr. Hogan liked his salesmen to have knowledge of their products. One year, he sent me to a sales school in Youngstown, Ohio, and I stayed up there for a week attending General Fireproofing training school's "Curriculum on Product Knowledge and Sales Techniques." We met in a school-like facility at the GF factory. It was interesting. And since I had to sell their products, I think it was important I learned how to show my customers how a chair was made, and why they made it a certain way. This also gave me the opportunity to have the knowledge to share a little bit about the history of the company. I had a good time up there, and I met a lot of people from other parts of the US. I was grateful to Mr. Hogan for opportunities like that, where I could learn more about products we were presenting to customers."

Royal made a lot of friends in other businesses—all of them customers—who helped him participate in other ventures that helped him financially.

JACQUE: *Daddy met influential people like the Moncriefs, who were in the oil business,*

Royal Hogan, center front, with part of the sales staff.
Don Bassham is on the back row, left.
Courtesy of Don Bassham.

and others in the real estate business, and he would invest in ventures with them. He was also a firm believer in making friends and contacts on the golf course, to aid his own business or gain access to possible investments.

Royal would also purchase memberships for his key employees at various golf courses so that they could carry on business in an entertaining setting.

Don recalls fondly, "Mr. Hogan bought a membership for me and my family at Diamond Oaks—that's where we lived. He had friends out in Diamond Oaks, and customers as well. Mr. Selman, who was a purchasing agent at the bank in Diamond Oaks, encouraged Mr. Hogan to get a membership, so he gave it to me. It was a company membership providing me the opportunity to play golf with current or potential customers. It turned out that I probably didn't bring as much business in as people think you can do belonging to a country club, but at the same time, I got to meet a lot of people, and it was good for my family. Mr. Hogan knew that. We had it [the club membership] for twenty-five years, and Mr. Hogan always paid the membership dues. I recall Mr. Hogan also bought a membership at Ridglea Country Club for Jack Clemons about the same time he bought mine at Diamond Oaks."

Royal was an astute businessman, but he was set in his ways. When someone called the store and asked to speak to Mr. Hogan, it was his rule that whoever answered would put the call directly through without asking who was calling.

JACQUE: *To Daddy, this was important. Courtesy was expected, and he felt everyone should be treated with respect. No one who answered at the store was to ask who was on the phone, just put the call through to the person requested. He refused to be rude to any customer. You were either there or you weren't there—it was very old school. I think his customers really appreciated that.*

Every year Royal would take two or three of his key employees to trade conventions in Chicago. They would stay at fine hotels like the old Stevens Hotel or occasionally at the Chicago Club, where Royal's friend Earl Baldridge was a member. Sometimes, if they happened to be going in that direction, the Moncriefs would fly Royal and his salesmen

in their airplane to Chicago. This was a very large plane, with a full-time pilot and copilot, and occasionally Tex would let his pilots take the Hogan entourage to and from the conventions without them.

Don recalled, "Those were wonderful times and memories. It was a little work and a lot of fun! A vacation for Mr. Hogan and those of us lucky enough to be included every year."

The Fort Worth Office Supply salesmen loved these trips with their boss, as they stayed at nice places and ate at Mr. Hogan's favorite restaurants, like downtown's Don the Beachcomber or the Rib, a dive joint on the north side with the best pork ribs in Chicago. Royal even took his employees to the horse races on their off time.

The conventions were usually at McCormick Place on Michigan Avenue. They would make the rounds visiting the displays of General Fireproofing, National Blank Book, and many other companies such as Wallace Pencil, Carter's Ink, Schaeffer and Parker Pen, and Royal Chair, which supplied products for Fort Worth Office Supply.

Don Bassham remembers fondly his boss's love of horse races, good food, and visiting with his suppliers at the conventions. Don recalls, "Mr. Hogan loved to look at things and loved to order all types of new products. As we would walk through McCormick Place

Present-day photo of the original building housing
Joe T. Garcia's restaurant in Fort Worth.
Photo by Peter Barbour.

showrooms, Mr. Hogan made decisions very fast. If he liked a product and thought it would sell, he bought it and would have it shipped to Fort Worth. After we were through with the displays for the day, Mr. Hogan would invite us out for cocktail hour at one of the fine downtown hotels."

When Royal and the sales staff returned to Fort Worth, packages of new products purchased in Chicago would be waiting for them to display in the store. The newer, modern office furniture provided a new niche for the salesmen to approach their customer base once again. The trade convention trips more than paid for their expense each year from the growing sales of the most recent models of office equipment and furniture.

The Hogans didn't entertain much, but during football season they would have some employees over for drinks before the games. Then, they would all climb into Royal's Cadillac and drive to the TCU football stadium. Royal parked in his reserved space directly behind their seats.

Don recalled, "My wife, Nelda, and I would go to their home from time to time. Mrs. Hogan always enjoyed Nelda being there, and they would visit. I remember Mrs. Hogan as an unusual person. She stayed in mostly, didn't really like to socialize in public as I recall, but she always made sure that everything was okay at home for Mr. Hogan.

On those Saturdays during football season, Mrs. Hogan liked to offer us something to eat or something to drink before we went over to the TCU stadium, about a block away from their house. It seemed that Mrs. Hogan was always doing something nice for us. I was invited to several Christmas parties, most of which were at David and Jacque Corley's beautiful home, and it was nice for us because we had never been anyplace like that with bartenders and waitresses serving the food and drinks. They treated my wife and me just like family. Sometimes we would meet the Hogans at Joe T. Garcia's to eat."

Joe T. Garcia's, which is located on the north side near the stockyards, opened on July 4, 1935. It was originally called Joe T.'s BBQ and Mexican Dishes, but the name was soon changed to Joe T. Garcia's when the family decided to concentrate solely on Mexican dishes. Royal and his family were fixtures at that landmark Mexican restaurant every Sunday at 5 p.m.

The Hogan family always sat at the same table in a small front room by the window. They would enter through the kitchen and greet Joe and his wife, "Mama" Garcia, who did all of the cooking. They would exit the kitchen, pass by the icebox, grab a beer or soda, and say "hello" to the parrot that sat in its perch in the small alcove. One of the Garcia's young daughters, Josephine, Pauline,

LEFT TO RIGHT: Sisters Mary, Josephine, Hope, and Pauline
with father Joe T. Garcia at the cash register on the opening
day of the restaurant, July 4, 1935.
Courtesy of Joe T. Garcia's.

Present-day view of the gardens at Joe T. Garcia's.
Photo by Peter Barbour.

Mary and Jacque stand at Royal's table in the front room where Mary used to serve the Hogans.
Photo by Peter Barbour.

Mary, or Hope, would greet them, and the Hogans would take a seat at their usual table. Chips and salsa were delivered by one of the sisters, and then came the dinner. Joe T.'s was unique in that it did not have menus; it only served one dinner, consisting of two enchiladas, rice, beans, guacamole, a beef taco, and tortillas served family style. At the end of the meal, all of the empty sodas and beer bottles would be left on the table, and one of the girls would count them to figure out the bill.

JACQUE: *I started going there when I was six years old. It was a ritual that as soon as my daddy finished playing golf every Sunday, he would pick us up to go to Joe T.'s. He always liked to get there as close to 5 p.m. as possible, because that was when they opened. One time when we walked in, some people were sitting at our table, and my daddy went over and said very politely, "You're sitting at my table." The couple got up and moved without saying anything. Daddy was always such a creature of habit.*

Joe T. Garcia's daughter Mary recalled, "One Sunday our family was at a picnic in Trinity Park, and we were having such a good time that my Dad had us stay an extra half-hour. We returned to the restaurant at 5:30, and Mr. Hogan and his family, who had been waiting for at least thirty minutes, were standing by the kitchen door. I remember Mr. Hogan giving us a stern look and saying, 'You're late.' It just happened that one time. Mr. Hogan was our best customer for years and years."

Royal also liked to go to lunch at Joe T.'s. He would walk over to the Moncrief Oil Company's office building almost every day at noon to have lunch with W. A. and Tex. Sometimes, they would eat in, with lunch served by the Moncrief's chef, or they might go out to River Crest or over to the Fort

Hope and Pauline Garcia with a platter of enchiladas.
Courtesy of Joe T. Garcia's.

Worth Club and later the Petroleum Club, but their all-time favorite was Joe T.'s. They usually made sure to go there once a week. And they took their own cheese.

Royal's grandson, Dr. David Corley Jr., remembers: "They didn't like the cheese, so Tex and Royal would take their own cheese, Cracker Barrel I believe, and have them make the enchiladas or tacos with their cheese. They ate lunch there all of the time, and then my mother and my grandparents went there every Sunday forever."

As David's wife, Dayna Corley, reflected, "It was always fun to go with Pops to Joe T.'s, because they always had a table for him. People would wait for hours, but Pops could go in through the kitchen and they *always* had his table."

JACQUE: *The Garcias loved Mr. Monty, Tex, and Daddy. They were three of the steadiest customers over the years. It was always, how are you Mr. Moncrief, Mr. Hogan—anything you need? And, the great respect with which they were treated by the Garcia family was returned by the Moncriefs and the Hogans, who were faithful patrons of the restaurant for over forty years.*

Royal's idiosyncrasies weren't restricted to his eating habits, as Jacque remembers very well. His control over his family and his company was ever present. On a recent visit to Colonial Country Club, Scott Corpening, a fellow member, approached Jacque and related a story that described Royal's control technique. Scott's father had an oil company that was a customer of Hogan Fort Worth Office Supply. Tragically, Scott's father and six other people who worked for him were killed in a plane crash, so Scott returned to Fort Worth to run the business his father had started.

Scott recalled, "I had a couple of good friends of mine, Wally Green and Bob Wood, who happened to have an office supply business—Greenwood Office Supply. They were my age and just starting out. Soon after I took over the business, a salesman named Don Bassham, who worked for Mr. Hogan, dropped in on me. I mentioned I was thinking of quitting Hogan's to buy from my buddies, to help support them, and get them off the ground. Well, Don said, 'Did we do something wrong?' I said, 'No.' I thought no one could be worried about our account. . . . We were a little bitty oil concern."

Fort Worth Office Supply worried about every account. Don mentioned this to Scott, and then informed him that Mr. Hogan wanted to visit with him.

Scott laughed, "He wasn't talking about Mr. Hogan coming to our office and visiting—I had been summoned to the corner of Houston and Eighth. We were about a block or so from there, so I walked down to their offices and I was literally terrified. His office was in the back of the store, and I walked in, told one of the sales staff who I was, and they ushered me back to his office. I shook hands with Mr. Hogan and we had some pleasantries. Then at one point, he said something like, 'Your dad was a fine young man and he was on his way to bigger and better things. What a tragedy.' I knew the hammer was in his hand—I just didn't know when it was going to drop. Finally, Mr. Hogan said, 'I understand we have new people, new faces, and all that, but I worked hard to earn your dad's trust and feel like we've done a good job, and until we don't do a good job, I expect your continued alliance. Now, I understand you have friends who you're trying to support, but they're younger than I am, and you can support them when I am through.' Needless to say, our business went back to him after one order from my buddies. From then on, absolutely every order went back to Mr. Hogan."

In the early 1960s Fort Worth Office Supply went through a period of transition and transformation. A New York City architectural and design firm, Skidmore, Owings & Merrill, revolutionized the entire office design industry by making offices more attractive and workable. General Fireproofing, who had built furniture based on the firm's designs, approached customers like Fort Worth Office Supply and suggested they hire designers to redesign offices.

Jacque and her first husband, David Corley, had returned from Madrid, Spain, in 1959, after David had finished a four-year stint in the air force. They had met at SMU, where both studied interior design. David recalled, "When we returned to Fort Worth, office suppliers, especially in Dallas, were hiring designers. So, because of my background, Mr. Hogan hired me to bring a design element to his business. I say background—I'm sure it helped I was his son-in-law."

David first went to work selling products to familiarize himself with the lines. Then he created the interior design department, and Jacque would join him with her design concepts. David developed a new logo that concentrated on the name Hogan more than on Fort Worth, so it was at about this time that Fort Worth Office Supply began to be known as the Hogan Office Supply Company.

Don Bassham recalls, "Mr. Hogan encouraged us to use their interior design department and sell new lines of furniture from GF and the very nice, modern furniture from Mies van der Rohe. Those new lines were hard to sell for an office supply salesman like myself, because I wasn't familiar with the design aspects. I learned more as I got to work with David Corley and Jacque through the design department. It was a real good time to include a successful interior design team, and that enabled us to become very successful in the office design and furniture business. We were competing with firms like Stationers—they did a lot of this type of work. But we had a man on the floor who would go out and meet the customers and explain what we could make their office look like, and David did a real good job."

Hogan Office Supply's first big interior design job was the Union Bank's brand new building in downtown Fort Worth. David and Jacque picked out the carpet, the wall colors, pictures for the walls, and working with Don or Jack, they would order the appropriate desks, chair mats, office chairs, benches, file cabinets, and anything else that was needed. It was a collaborative effort involving the whole company, and it proved to be very successful, leading to many other office redesigns or interior makeovers for years to come. When David and Jacque started with the company, it was estimated that 25 percent of the business came from furniture, and 75 percent was from the various supplies. After a few years with the design elements in place and customers warming to the idea of change, the profits reversed, with almost 80 percent of the business coming from the design/furniture area.

David remembers it as hard work and some long hours, but it was also fun. Each new job proved to be a new experience and provided its own set of problems or situations that were different from previous jobs. And, in spite of the long hours, David enjoyed working for Royal.

David remembered, "He was a great guy to work for. If you worked hard, he'd take care of you. He wouldn't keep you around if you didn't work hard. He was honest. He never bought cheap supplies, staples for example, and then mark them up. He was fair to his employees and loyal to his customers. He worked hard. So we did, too."

JACQUE: *David was a decorator, and he was very good at what he did. But, without the help of people like Don, Jack Clemons, Arch Boulware, and Glen Little, David couldn't have pulled it off. Don would go measure the chairs, the chair mats, and you had to know what you were doing to order the right chair with the right detail. David did not have that expertise, as his position was the overview, the decorating, the color, making it look pretty. But, when it came down to the details, it took people like Don.*

Don adds, "Sometimes, when we were out in the field calling on a customer, we would take David or Jacque with us to suggest a change to this type of chair or that type of furniture, and that was a big help. But, for the most part, we would take our brochures and catalogs and would order everything from the factories. Once you tied up a customer with this all-encompassing service, and you satisfied them, which we did, you would get all of their business. And Jack, Arch, and I knew our customers."

Bill Denkins, a media advertising salesman for a local radio station in the 1960s, remembers selling Royal on drive-time spots, morning and afternoon rush hours, for Hogan Office Supply advertising. Bill recalls, "They would be 'broad spots,' general in nature, short and to the point. And then, every year during the Colonial tournament, Royal would sponsor the *Tournament Report*, where the station would break into its regular programming to report the scores from the course."

The collaboration of the design team, the salesmen, advertising, and Royal's leadership led to a very profitable decade for Hogan Office Supply Company. Then, in 1963, in order to make room for the new convention center, the City of Fort Worth condemned Royal's store at 1007 Main Street. This would be the fourth time Royal moved his business, and he was determined it would be his last. He purchased an empty lot east of the courthouse on Belknap Street with the intention of building a new store, but abandoned construction when he discovered another prime location. It was a perfect-sized three-story building at 901 Houston Street. McCrory's, a variety store, had vacated the building, which was one block from the new Moncrief Oil Company office building. Royal purchased the property at 901 Houston, then applied for and received a historical marker. Royal felt this recognition would protect him from ever having to relocate again.

Royal had asked David Corley and Mr. Dingler to take charge of remodeling the new building so that it would be efficient for deliveries, comfortable for the staff, and pleasant to the eye of those customers who came to the store. Royal hired a carpenter, Spencer Kean, to aid in the renovations.

The key part of the new store was to be on the ground floor, divided into one section for office supplies and one section showcasing the various furniture lines, arranged into office suites for display. At the back of the main floor was Royal's large executive office, with a glass window so he could look out on the showroom and curtains that could be drawn for privacy. Directly in front of Royal's office was David Corley's decorating section, with a large glass conference table used for displaying carpet, paint, and fabric samples. There were also catalogs of all of the furniture lines Hogan Office Supply represented. The desks for the secretaries, accountant, and several bookkeepers were on a balcony overlooking the main floor. The second and third floors were used for storage of large, bulk packages of office supplies. The building had an

Hogan Office Supply building at 901 Houston Street.
Photo by Robert Towery.

entrance on the side on Eighth Street, and from there one could go left and down to the basement, or up a couple of steps to the rear of the store, where there was a freight elevator that also opened out to the alley behind the store for loading and unloading large pieces of furniture.

Royal was very happy with the design of the basement, where there was a kitchen with a sink, a refrigerator, a stove, and an area where employees could have lunch and take a break. Directly below the glass-squared patchwork sidewalk was an overstock room that stored pencils, paper, erasers, and other small office supplies. The basement also included an area that displayed various office furniture, chairs, tables, lamps, file cabinets, and other items. One floor below was a grey-painted sub-basement housing the air conditioning and heating systems. All of the equipment in the sub-basement was painted hot pink. The final touch was replacing all of the light fixtures and fans throughout the building. The new lights were globes, twenty inches in diameter, which hung down from the metal ceiling eighteen feet above.

Royal hired a local artistic painter, Howard Thompson, to paint the inside and outside of the building. He chose beige for the outside, and he painted a very unusual eighteen-inch rust-colored stripe entirely around the building. After all the renovations were completed, the new store was ready to be occupied.

Salesman Don Bassham reflected on how they moved everything from the Main Street location to the new Houston Street location as one of the smoothest, most organized transitions one could ever realize. The staff knew exactly where everything would go in the new building. The move was like a precise military maneuver that the employees of Hogan Office Supply Company accomplished in a couple of days.

Royal decided to throw a grand opening for his customers, suppliers, and the public at large, for he wanted to show off his new store. He was very proud of it.

JACQUE: *We did business in the morning. Daddy wouldn't shut down for a little grand opening. But in the afternoon, foot traffic slowed a little and it was more casual. Mother was there all day, which was quite a surprise. After 5:00 we served cocktails. It was a huge success, and Daddy loved it!*

A beautiful rust-colored metal sign, "Hogan Office Supply Co.," suspended from the back roof of the building (which still stands) could be seen from the corner of Eighth and Main Street, and from the plaza in front of the famous Hotel Texas (now the Hilton). Royal's business settled in at the new location, and armed with a new motto—"If Used in an Office, We Have It!"—the company was primed for continued growth and success.

12

THE HOGAN SLAM

In 1952, Ben continued to experience a lot of pain in his legs, so he cut back his schedule and entered only three of the tour's seventy-two-hole tournaments—the Masters, the Colonial NIT, and the US Open at Northwood Country Club in Dallas. He had really wanted to play in the Crosby Pro Am on the Monterrey Peninsula, but he felt the dampness and cold that enveloped that event would be too hard on him. Out of his three tour appearances in 1952, his only victory for the year came at Colonial.

After winning the 1951 Masters, Ben approached the tournament's host, the legendary Bobby Jones, and suggested that the previous champions should gather for a dinner prior to the tournament each year. So in 1952, Ben hosted the start of one of Augusta's most famous traditions, the Masters Club, which evolved into the Champions Dinner that is still held every year. In the tournament following that first dinner, after three rounds, Ben was tied with Sam Snead. But on Sunday, strong winds and cool temperatures affected Ben's condition. He struggled to a 79, losing to Snead by seven strokes.

The Colonial NIT that year was held from May 22 through May 25, and the total purse for the tournament had been raised to $20,000, matching it with the Masters. Rain postponed the second round, so the golfers would have to play thirty-six holes on Sunday.

After the morning round, Raymond Gafford, who lived in Fort Worth, was the surprise leader with a five-stroke lead over Ben. As he played in the final group, the pressure got to the young leader, and he collapsed to a round of 80. Playing really well and demonstrating excellent putting, Ben shot a 67, winning the tournament by four strokes, and taking home the winner's share of $4,000.

Though Ben would play in several one-day golf exhibitions, the final of his three seventy-two-hole events for 1952 was forty miles east of his beloved Colonial, down US Hwy 67 at the Northwood Club in Dallas. Completed over three hot Texas summer days, from June 12 through June 14, this was only the second time the USGA had hosted a US Open in the South. Ben was a two-time defending champion and seeking to match Willie Anderson to be one of the only two players to win three consecutive Opens. Anderson, the famed Scottish golfer, had won the US Open from 1903–1905.

Unfortunately, it was not to be. Even after Ben took a two-shot lead after thirty-six holes, he had to play the final thirty-six on Saturday in the oppressive Dallas heat. The near 100-degree temperatures exhausted Ben, and he shot a couple of 74s, while Julius Boros posted an excellent final day of 68 and 71 to win the 52nd Open by four strokes.

Ben was done for the year, except of course to continue to "dig it out of the dirt." For the rest of 1952, he returned to Colonial's practice range every day that he was in Fort Worth. When 1953 arrived, Ben was in top form, and after some more practice and warmup rounds at the Seminole Country Club with his good friend George Coleman, he was full of confidence and ready to play to the best of his ability. It didn't surprise him at all that he started his 1953 tour season with a four-shot victory at Augusta. Ben's four-day Masters total of fourteen under par broke the tournament's scoring record by five strokes, and would not be matched for another twelve years.

Then in April of 1953, fire destroyed the Colonial's clubhouse. It was the second time in ten years that a fire had ravaged the building, but this time around, the inferno completely destroyed the famed white wooden structure. Royal Hogan was among the members who rushed to the scene, but like the others already there, he could do nothing to stop the flames.

JACQUE: *Daddy heard all of the fire engines, and he knew it was something big, because it was so close. He jumped in the car because he thought it was the club and drove over there. Club members had formed a line passing the golf bags one after another out of the building, looking a little like the water bucket brigades fighting flames in the old*

The Colonial clubhouse, completely destroyed after the
second devastating fire in 1953. The members saved all
of the golf clubs and bags.
Courtesy FWST/UTA.

days. But they weren't putting out the fire— they were saving their golf clubs.

After winning again a few weeks later at the Pan American Open, and a short five weeks after the fire, Ben returned to the original Hogan's Alley to defend his title at Colonial. With tents and temporary buildings in place for the tournament, Ben destroyed the rest of the field in the NIT, winning at Colonial for the fourth time in six attempts. His final round in Marvin Leonard's Invitational was a beautiful 67 in severe winds, to come back and win the championship by five shots. It was an excellent round of golf with an eagle and three birdies against two bogies. The winds had been so gnarly that Jimmy Demaret withdrew after nine holes in the second round, when he reached seventeen over par for the tournament.

JACQUE: *I was twenty years old in 1953, and I followed Uncle Ben for the entire eighteen holes the final round. It was one of those legendary days at Colonial when the winds were really blowing hard. I was walking among the gallery, and nobody knew who I was or that I had any connection to Ben Hogan. The entire eighteen holes I would hear one after another of the fans talking about Uncle Ben, his swing, his comeback, his courage—it was so much fun for me to be hearing the various people talk so affectionately about my uncle. I never heard anything negative, it was all*

sincere praise and heartfelt opinions, and it really made me feel proud I was a Hogan.

Another thread in Colonial history was introduced in 1953, when the tournament committee invited Fort Worth native Byron Nelson to hit the first ball off the first tee. Lord Byron had retired at the peak of his career after the 1946 season because he had made enough money in professional golf to follow his real dream of becoming a rancher on land he had purchased northwest of Dallas. Ben Hogan lost one of his fiercest competitors on the tour when Lord Byron retired, but the two Fort Worth legends remained friends for the rest of their lives. The tradition of Mr. Nelson hitting the first ball of the Colonial NIT continued for many years.

Oakmont Country Club, located in a suburb northeast of Pittsburgh, Pennsylvania, was the USGA's site for the 1953 US Open. Ben was on a roll and opened with a five-under par 67. He would become the first player since 1921 to lead after every round. His six-stroke victory over second place Sam Snead was the largest margin of victory at a US Open in fifteen years.

As the year moved forward, Ben had a decision to make. The 1953 PGA Championship would be held July 1 through July 7 in Birmingham, Michigan. It required two qualifying rounds in one day, and then six rounds of match play over five straight days. So much walking up and down on a golf course was not recommended, and perhaps impossible, given Ben's condition. The British Open almost overlapped the PGA Championship in 1953, and was to be held at Carnoustie, Scotland, from July 8 through July 10. Given the travel venues of the day, it would be impossible to play both tournaments.

JACQUE: *Uncle Ben had never seriously considered playing in the British Open. He hated flying and dreaded the weather that threatened to give him so much trouble with his legs. Also, he did not want to be that far from home and didn't care for the smaller golf ball used in that Open championship.*

ROBERT: *Deep inside, the challenge was always there and tempting Ben, but at this stage in his life he did not believe he had anything to prove to anyone except himself. Therein lay the kicker. A lot of golfers and the press were encouraging him to go to Scotland. I think Valerie put a lot of pressure on him, and not for all the right reasons. Finally, he decided to enter the British Open, and the press went wild. Privately, he made up his mind to go over early, stay for a while and adjust to the weather, practice often, and then win. For he knew he would not come back.*

Ben and Valerie went "over the pond" on the SS United States, arriving in Carnoustie a couple of weeks before the Open championship began. Ben made reservations at the Bruce Hotel near the Carnoustie links, but when they arrived the accommodations did not meet their requirements. There were no rooms with a private bath except for one large suite, which was still unacceptable because of Ben's special needs, so he refused it.

JACQUE: *Uncle Ben had to soak his legs in a tub of warm water for an hour or two each day, so he had to have a large bath in his room.*

Ben was about ready to forget the Open and return to the United States. A well-connected friend intervened, however, and Ben was offered the use of a private residence, Tay Park. It was owned by National Cash Register. NCR maintained Tay Park on the outskirts of Dundee, where it owned a manufacturing plant. The corporation used the beautiful estate for entertaining company officials, traveling customers, and business executives. Ben decided to accept the offer. As it turned out, the residence was much more comfortable than a hotel for Ben and Valerie, who loved being doted on by the resident staff.

JACQUE: *Uncle Ben could hardly believe how nice it was, especially with its cordial employees and its big beautiful bathroom with a big tub.*

ROBERT: *Ben was not as impressed with the layout of Carnoustie at his first sighting of the course, though he grew to understand*

and appreciate its idiosyncrasies. As he would later write, "Heather and gorse are abundant in the rough. Heather, something like a fern, grows in clumps about eight inches to a foot high and as thick as it can be. If you get in it, you have to hit the ball about ten times as hard as you would otherwise, and then most times it won't go more than ten yards or so. I was in it only once, thank goodness, and that was during a qualifying round. It was up close to a green and fortunately I came out of it all right. Gorse is taller, sometimes waist-to-head high, and is a brambly bush. I don't know what you do if you get into it, and I never wanted to find out. I didn't practice getting out of the gorse or heather because I figured anyone who would get into it frequently wouldn't have a chance anyway."

Ben had been assigned a local caddy and they began to practice together. Because summers were so long in Scotland, Ben could practice late into the evening. He practiced every day at Panmure Golf Club, a links course similar to Carnoustie, and just a couple of miles down the road from where the Open championship would be contested. He also played several rounds at Carnoustie to help him formulate his plans for managing the golf ball around the course. He knew he had to avoid the heather, gorse, and numerous sand traps that were sometimes in the center of the fairways.

ROBERT: *Ben wrote, "I believed after two weeks of practice that the tee shot would be the most important because of the course and the weather and thought that a score of 283 would win it. I did a lot of practicing with wood clubs, more than I normally do for tournaments."* I found it was interesting and revealing that Ben Hogan had two weeks to prepare for a golf course, and especially that year with how he had been playing. I figured he thought that if he understood the proper location and placement of his shots around Carnoustie, that in his positive way of thinking, the Open championship was his for the taking.

When the tournament time arrived, Ben was ready. He shot 73-71-70-68 for a 282 total, at that time the lowest score ever in a British Open, and won by four shots over fellow American and amateur Frank Stranahan and three others. Ben's 68 in the final round was a course record at Carnoustie. Ben won the respect of the British fans, who had all grown fond of calling him by his affectionate Scottish nickname, the Wee Ice Man. Ben had also made a lasting impression on Carnoustie itself. Its par-five sixth hole had a split fairway, with the right side wider and safer, but the left side offered a much better approach to the green. In all four rounds, Ben's drives on the sixth hole found the center of the left side of the fairway, and this

1953 Ticker-tape parade honors Ben for his unbelievable
achievement of the Hogan Slam.
Copyright Bettman/Corbis / AP Images.

was a key in his victory. The hole has since
been known as "Hogan's Alley," the third
landmark golf course to honor the great golfer. And who could argue that Ben Hogan was
one of the best who ever played the game?

With his victory, Ben became the only
golfer to win the Masters, US Open, and British Open Championship in one calendar year,
and he was only the second golfer to capture
all four major titles in a career, matching Gene
Sarazen, who had accomplished the feat in
the 1920s and 30s. Ben had won five of the
six tournaments he had entered in 1953, and
the three major victories in a row became
known as the "Hogan Slam." Returning to
New York City, his achievements were celebrated with a ticker-tape parade on July 21,
1953—twenty-three years after the only other golfer, Bobby Jones, had been so honored.

13

THE BEN HOGAN COMPANY

"There is no similarity between golf and putting.
. . . They are two different games. One played
in the air, the other on the ground."

— BEN HOGAN

After the Manhattan ticker-tape parade, Ben and Valerie planned to fly from New York City to Dallas's Love Field. They changed their plans, however, and landed at Carter Field in Fort Worth after a city leader contacted Ben and informed him that the city had formed a committee to set up a two-day celebration in his honor. Ben's friends and various Fort Worth movers and shakers, led by Mayor Edgar Deen, wished to honor their most distinguished citizen. They planned a simple ceremony to greet and con-gratulate Ben in the terminal of the airport, followed the next day by a downtown luncheon in the Crystal Ballroom at the Hotel Texas, where six hundred tickets had been presold to the public.

When Ben and Valerie arrived at Carter Field, they were very surprised by the number of people waiting to greet them. As they descended the stairs and stepped onto a red carpet stretching from the plane to the terminal, Valerie was presented with a large bouquet of flowers. Ben, wearing a huge smile, took

Mama Hogan stands proudly next to the Colonial trophy in an exhibit of trophies in a Fort Worth bank lobby in 1953, after Ben won the Masters, US Open, and British Open in one calendar year. JHT family collection.

off his hat and waved at the crowd. The Carswell Air Force Base band started playing the "Eyes of Texas" as Ben and Valerie strolled down the red carpet lined by military guardsmen. As they continued toward the terminal, they passed between hostesses holding placards that spelled, "Welcome Home Hogan." There was a double line of Fort Worth police officers holding back an enthusiastic throng of supporters and fans. They entered the terminal and were greeted by Mama Hogan. Photographers asked for a picture, and the one that appeared in the papers the next day showed Ben and his mother, arms around each other's backs, with a man holding a huge Scottish Flag behind them. The man was J. O. (Captain) Kidd, of Scottish descent. He had been the manager of Glen Garden Country Club when Ben was a caddy there many years before.

Also in the throng to meet the returning conquering hero were Royal, Margaret, Jacque, and Valerie's sister Sarah Harriman. Ben and Valerie were escorted to a small stage, where city dignitaries, including Mayor Deen, were waiting to greet them. The mayor approached the lectern, welcomed Ben home, and congratulated him on his "Grand Slam." Applause and cheers broke out from the throng. After the din of excitement waned, Mayor Deen said, "Ben, you were a poor boy who came up the hard way, and that's why we love you all the more." More applause filled the north end of the Carter Field terminal. The mayor stepped away from the lectern and asked if Ben wanted to say a few words.

Ben stepped forward, choked back emotion, and spoke softly, "I don't think anybody ever had people pulling for them so hard as we did. God bless you all." He paused and looked around the area, acknowledging many familiar faces, shrugged his shoulders, and added, "You know, we would have made better time if we'd gone to Love Field." He grinned and added, "They prevailed on me to come to Fort Worth, and I am glad we landed here. Thank you all."

In the press conference that followed a little later, Ben told those assembled that before going to Scotland, he had American manufacturers produce golf balls that were the size specified by the British Golf Association. The British ball was smaller than the American version. He said, "You get a sort of mushy feel with the British ball." He was more accustomed to the "feel" of the American ball, and the smaller American ball he had manufactured worked out pretty well for him at Carnoustie.

Ben then surprised everyone when he announced he had become involved with some experiments that might revolutionize the manufacture of golf clubs. He believed that if he and his unnamed associates were successful, they would build a factory. He said they would be making their decision soon; perhaps after he returned from a fishing trip to Canada, his first real restful vacation in several years, he might have further news.

Ben had a very wealthy friend, A. Pollard Simons, who had made a fortune with his Simons Land Company in Dallas. Back in 1948, the two were thinking about building a golf course together in the Coachella Valley in California. They flew out to see if they could find a site for a golf course and were introduced to Johnny Dawson, who was already in the process of planning a golf course for the valley. Dawson, an executive with A. G. Spalding, had vacationed in the Palm Springs area the previous year and decided to stay and develop a golf resort. He conducted surveys and found water sources were plentiful from the snow melting off the nearby mountains and the underwater rivers flowing below the valley. Dawson purchased the 182-acre Thunderbird Dude Ranch and was starting to look for investors when he met Ben Hogan and Pollard Simons. Learning of their plans, he decided he didn't want competition from a Hogan-Simons planned course, so he asked the two to join him in the Thunderbird venture. Dawson took Simons and Ben out to the site of the Thunderbird, and when Ben saw that the site was nothing more than sand and brush he was dismayed. He told Dawson, "You'll never build a golf course out here."

Dawson then joined Ben and Simons as a minor member of their group, and the three began a search for a good site. They found a location about ten miles north of Palm Springs with fertile dunes, a solid growth of vegetation, and water just below the surface. Ben thought it would be perfect and returned to Fort Worth while Simons and Dawson remained behind to contact the owner of the land to negotiate a purchase. A couple of days before the sale was expected to close, Simons and Dawson took a final trip out to look at the acreage they were buying. A huge desert wind began to howl, and when they arrived on the site there was so much dust and sand in the air they couldn't even see the dunes. Simons decided building a golf course out in this barren desert probably wasn't a good idea, and he returned to Dallas. Dawson, back on his own, found another partner and ended up building his Thunderbird Country Club on the original site of the dude ranch. It would be the first golf course in the Coachella Valley, an area of California that is now a Mecca for golfers in the western United States.

In 1953, Ben approached Simons with another idea for an investment, a golf equipment factory to produce a new design of irons and woods. They formed a partnership, and the Ben Hogan Company was formed in the fall of 1953. The partnership didn't last very long, however. When the first set of irons manufactured at their new factory at 2930 West Pafford Street did not measure up to Ben's exacting standards, he threw them out—at a cost of one hundred thousand dollars. Simons was upset, but Ben didn't care. He wanted it done right . . . perfectly . . . or else not at all. Simons kept objecting, saying, "We can fix them up."

Upset by his partner's motives, Ben bought Simons out right then and there. When he got home that night, he told Valerie, "I lost a partner, but I kept my integrity. I would never put those clubs on sale. I can't do that to people and I'm not going to do it."

In his search for other financial backing, Ben approached another wealthy man for investment in his company, one he knew would believe in him.

As Marty Leonard remembers, "Ben approached my daddy and asked him if he would help with the financing. He helped him, of course. I think Daddy would have originally, but Pollard Simons had stepped up to back Ben in the beginning. That didn't work out, and they parted ways. Ben was a perfectionist."

So, with Marvin Leonard's backing, and that of a few other investors he attracted—

The building on Pafford Street where the
Ben Hogan Company was located.
Photo by Robert Towery.

their friend Bing Crosby among them—the Ben Hogan Company was on its way. From its inception, Ben's striving for perfection led to the manufacturing of some of the best golf equipment available. But it wasn't necessarily for the professional that Ben was building his clubs. He was building them for the amateurs as well, who didn't have access to the skillfully designed golf clubs that the pros had custom made. Ben always wanted his equipment to be of exceptional quality, and also to meet the needs of every golfer. He believed at the time, and it was later justified, that the amateur player would appreciate a set of precisely matched clubs built to what Ben called "the most exacting tolerances modern machinery will allow. There are no shortcuts in the quest for perfection."

In 1954, the Ben Hogan Company's first set of "Precision Irons" were manufactured and distributed to country club pro shops. They were an instant success. Golfers, pro and amateur alike, were very pleased with their feel and touch. The next year, at the 1955 US Open at the Olympic Club in San Francisco, an unknown club pro named Jack Fleck defeated the great Ben Hogan in a playoff to win golf's national championship. Ironically, Fleck won his victory using the Precision irons of the Ben Hogan Company.

The company's engineers were always trying to find new designs for the next line of clubs. In 1957, the company introduced the aerodynamically efficient "Speed Slot" woods and drivers, featuring a totally new concept in club design. They had the familiar HOGAN etched into the metal strap on the bottom of the woods, and a crease in the toe of the persimmon head. These proved to be another very successful line of clubs and made the company very profitable.

JACQUE: *The Hogan line of women's golf clubs was called Princess after my aunt, Uncle Ben's dear older sister.*

One of Ben's long-time employees at the factory was a diminutive lady, Pat Martin, who was originally from Greenville, Texas. She had moved to Fort Worth after she married. In 1958, she went to work for Ben at his company. She held several positions over the years, starting out in customer service, then production control, and finally cost accounting. Pat then took a few years' leave to raise her children. When she returned to work, she took a position as one of Ben's secretaries, alongside Claribel Kelly. Ben and Royal had grown up with Claribel. Ben knew she had secretarial skills, and when he started the company, he asked Claribel if she would come to work for him. She did, and she stayed for thirty years.

Don Bassham, Royal's salesman, loved to call on the Ben Hogan Company at the Pafford Street factory. "Sometimes I would see Mr. Hogan," Don recalled, "but I dealt mostly with Claribel. I liked her—she always told me a joke. And then she would give me the order."

Claribel's nephew Mike Leman said of his aunt, "Claribel had a way of keeping Ben in line. They remained very close, and when my aunt passed away in 1986, Mr. Hogan served as one of her pallbearers."

Claribel's replacement was Doxie Williams, and Pat continued on assisting her with the secretarial chores. Pat worked for the Ben Hogan Company for twenty-nine years. These ladies, along with all of the employees of the company, loved working for Ben and were very loyal to him.

Pat remembers working for the Hogan Company with the utmost fondness, recalling,

Everything from Ben's office at the Ben Hogan Company was relocated to Colonial Country Club, in an area adjacent to the pro shop. Photo by Peter Barbour.

"I got along great with Mr. Hogan. He was so sweet; he could get along with anybody. One time when I was in production control, we had an order from a Japanese company that wanted shorter clubs. Well, when they came up for final inspection, they were the wrong size, about half an inch off. My immediate boss said, 'How in the hell am I going to explain this to Mr. Hogan?' I said, 'You won't have to; I will.' I went to Mr. Hogan's office, feeling it was my fault, and explained the situation. He just smiled and asked if I could get the customer on the phone. He convinced them these clubs, even though they were half an inch off the specs, would work just fine, and he guaranteed them. After he hung up, he smiled at me, 'It's all right—they're going to accept those clubs.'"

Royal would drop by Ben's factory every once in a while to talk. Pat recalled that during all of the years she worked at the company the two brothers would meet almost daily at Shady Oaks, but occasionally the older brother would drop by Ben's Pafford Street office.

Pat remembered, "Royal was a real gentleman. He would usually come in, take off his hat, and speak very cordially with Claribel and me, and then walk into Ben's office. However, there was one day that Royal showed up, and he didn't say a word to either of us. He didn't even remove his hat.

He just walked straight back to Ben's office, closed the door, and we heard some very loud talking, arguing you know, like brothers will do. We never knew what they were discussing, but it just happened that one time that I remember. Otherwise, they were always very respectful of each other. . . . They were very close."

In 1960, Ben sold his company to American Machine and Foundry (AMF), but he remained in charge as chairman of the board. During the sixties, the company flourished and continued to come up with new ideas for the manufacturing of golf equipment. Ben had always thought that one of the most important components of a golf club was the shaft. He was quoted as saying, "With a forged club, the feel goes right up the shaft, into your hands, and into your heart." He worked with his veteran club designer, Gene Sheely, to create and manufacture the first taper-tip steel shafts, which they named "Apex." They were instantly proclaimed the most consistent shafts to date. Then, a few years later, they designed the Apex irons, and the golfing public immediately praised them. Within a few years, the Apex irons were the most widely played irons on the PGA tour.

Pat Martin recalls, "When I went to work for Mr. Hogan, we had about eighty employees, and during the 1960s that number grew to five hundred. All kinds of people would drop in and visit our model shop for us to fit and make custom clubs for them. I remember one time Arnold Palmer dropped by the shop. Mr. Hogan was so excited to show him all around the plant. He explained to Mr. Palmer exactly how they made the clubs. He was so proud of his factory."

Ray Coleman started working for Ben at the Hogan Company in the 1960s and worked for him for nearly thirty years before going to work for Arnold Palmer. Ray started in the ball plant at the Hogan factory on Pafford Street, and then went into manufacturing and quality control. After a few years in quality control, Ray saw salesmen were making a lot more money, so he took a territory in upstate New York, then in Alabama and Tennessee. Finally, he became a district sales manager and ultimately national sales manager.

Ray recalls, "I reported directly to Mr. Hogan, whose blue-steel-gray eyes could cut right through you if you didn't have your facts straight. He always sought perfection in all of the work, no matter what it was. I witnessed him rejecting over 200 clubs because the Ben Hogan decal on the crown of the club was not attached correctly. There were approximately 185 different sets of operations to build a single golf club. We would work in lots—fifty five irons, then fifty six irons, and so forth. They would come down an

assembly line and each person had a specific job (like the lady who applied the decals). And knowing Mr. Hogan's penchant for perfection, one can imagine the pressure on the quality control division to make sure every step of the process was done correctly."

Ray remembers, "AMF had a wonderful association with Mr. Hogan. They let him run the company the way he wanted to. Nothing changed from 1953 into the 1980s as Mr. Hogan continued to control all aspects of manufacturing. Mr. Hogan hated when everything in retail started going to the big box stores. He didn't like that as a marketing approach. He liked the personal touch of salesmen calling on pro shops around the country. He had staff accounts with one hundred fifty PGA professionals—teaching, club, and tour pros—across the country, who worked for the Hogan Company. Their job was to promote Hogan golf products."

Every year, all sales representatives in the Hogan Company from the forty-eight regional territories would come to Fort Worth for a national sales meeting around August 13—Ben's birthday. He would sponsor the annual event at Colonial every year, and it was a real treat for the entire sales staff. They would have a big cake and everyone would sing "Happy Birthday" to their boss. In addition to the sales meeting, Ben would arrange for a salesmen's tournament at Colonial or Shady

Oaks.

Ray remembers fondly, "Ben Hogan never played a casual round of golf, and I should know, as practically every year I played with Mr. Hogan in the salesmen tournaments. Most of our salesmen were pretty good players. One year we played a fivesome at Shady Oaks, and Mr. Hogan was in a cart by himself with the Shady Oaks' dog, Buster, that he took care of when he was at the club. I played really well and shot a 72, and Mr. Hogan shot a 73. I asked him if he would sign the scorecard, and it was like pulling teeth. He didn't want to sign it, but eventually, he did. And I have had it framed on the wall in my office ever since."

Everyone who worked for Ben Hogan knew there was a right and a wrong way to do every aspect of the manufacturing, marketing, and sales process. And the right way was what all of his employees called the Hogan way.

Ray recalls, "There was an area in the grinding department in the bowels of the factory where you really didn't want to work. It was really hard job grinding down the metals. These workers got paid piecemeal, which meant they were paid by the number of pieces they made, and some of these guys were making a lot of money. As a quality control officer I made sure everything was done the right way, and the right way was the Hogan way. One morning I showed up, and Mr. Hogan's black Cadillac wasn't in his parking space, but parked near the back. I remember thinking we must have a situation. I go back to the bowels and find Mr. Hogan sitting behind two fellows who were grinding iron heads. There's a part called the notch that sets apart the shaft and the head of the golf club. Mr. Hogan had his hat on, coat, and tie, watching them grind away, and I walked back there and said, 'What's going on?' Mr. Hogan, holding up a head, said, 'These heads are Gawd-awful. You tell these fellows to go home since they can't do any better than this. And I mean right now.' I knew if I jumped their ass it would be better than if Mr. Hogan did, so I said I'd take care of it. Mr. Hogan walked away and I was relieved. I returned to my office, and after a moment Mr. Hogan came in, holding a bunch of the heads in his large hands. He was only five foot nine, but he had hands like catchers' mitts. Mr. Hogan stood there holding the heads and said, 'I told you these were Gawd-awful. I want to show you what I'm talking about.' And he threw the heads against the wall with a force that left dents that are probably still there today. I reached down to pick up the heads to inspect them, and they were too hot to touch. And Mr. Hogan had been carrying them for several minutes. His hands were so callused the intense heat hadn't bothered him."

For years, Ben Hogan had said, "Ray, call me Ben."

Ray would say, "Yes sir, Mr. Hogan."

Ray waxed philosophic when he summed up his time at the company, saying, "You know, I had a very wonderful life in the golf industry, and I traveled all over the world playing golf, and I don't remember ever having to pay a green fee. I thank the Hogan Company and especially Ben Hogan for making that happen."

After working for Ben Hogan, Ray went to work for Arnold Palmer at ProGroup, Incorporated, in Chattanooga, Tennessee. One night after a dinner meeting with executives of the company, Mr. Palmer asked Ray for a ride to his motel.

"It's ironic and sort of funny that he would fly up from his home in Orlando in his private jet, and instead of an elegant hotel (which would have been Mr. Hogan's preference), Mr. Palmer would stay at a Travelodge or another highway motel near the factory. As I drove Mr. Palmer to his room, he asked if I knew of a watering hole along the way where we could stop and share a beer. I called the manager of a TGIF-type bar I knew and told him I was bringing Arnold Palmer, and I wanted a quiet table in the back away from the crowd. When Mr. Palmer and I arrived, Arnie was instantly cheered and mobbed by the crowd in the bar. After he had signed au-

tographs for everyone, we settled in at our table. I ordered a Rusty Nail, and Mr. Palmer ordered a beer. After our drinks were delivered and we toasted the successes of the day, Mr. Palmer turned to me and asked, 'Ray, I need to know why Mr. Hogan chose to be the way he was around other people?'

"I replied, 'Well, he was a very private person. He didn't have the same outgoing personality that you present. I think he would have liked being more outgoing, but never was—just wasn't his nature.'

"Mr. Palmer then asked about Ben's business habits and the different way he ran his company. 'He was a perfectionist all the way,' I told him. 'For example, when he made a line of junior clubs, they were as exact and precisely manufactured as all of his products.'

"Mr. Palmer had several beers while I had a few Rusty Nails, and by the end of the evening, he was enamored of the Hogan style, and I think greatly admired his practice habits, his manner, his competitiveness, and his company. I'll never forget that evening when I got to spend a few hours with one of my favorite golfers of all time, talking about the magnificence and conundrum that was the great Ben Hogan."

14

SHADY OAKS AND THE HOGAN BROTHERS

At some point after Marvin Leonard had sold Colonial Country Club to its members in 1942, he began dreaming of building another golf course. Marvin's friend Amon Carter, the publisher of the *Fort Worth Star-Telegram*, had a ranch just west of Fort Worth, and he brought Marvin out to see if they could develop a golf course together on his land. But the two men could not agree on exactly where the course would be built, so they abandoned the idea. In June of 1955, Marvin took his family out to Pebble Beach for a vacation, and he began the process of looking for some land in California to develop a golf course. But fate stepped in to change his plans. Amon Carter had his sec-

ond heart attack in two years, and this time it was fatal. He passed away on June 23, 1955, at the age of seventy-six.

Marty Leonard recalls, "Apparently, Amon's will declared that when he died, his ranchland west of Fort Worth was to be offered to my dad first. We were in California, where we spent summers at Pebble Beach, and Daddy's attorney, Jenkins Garrett, called with the news. It did not take Daddy very long. There was no discussion about price, because he knew what he wanted to do with it. Daddy had almost bought some property near San Francisco, where he wanted to build another golf course in the worst way. So, we got on the train and came home, because

Daddy didn't like to fly. When we got home, the ranch was in the process of becoming my daddy's, and he immediately started planning Shady Oaks and its corresponding development."

Marvin would use his Cadillac like a truck, and he would drive all over the property, trying to envision the layout for the golf course and residential development. One day he brought Ben out to see it.

JACQUE: *Uncle Ben told me that he thought Mr. Marvin was a bit crazy to try and build a golf course on Mr. Carter's old ranch. He thought the countryside was too harsh, with too many hills for a golf course.*

Ben suggested that Marvin should discontinue his plans. Marvin—luckily, as Ben would admit later—didn't agree with his younger professional friend's opinion and decided to move forward with the project anyway. He was determined to build an ideal golf course and country club where the members would be treated like kings.

Marvin hired renowned golf architect Robert Trent Jones to design the golf course, and architects Hedrick & Stanley to create the clubhouse. Utilizing all of the machinery they could muster, the crew dug more dirt and leveled more land than on any previous golf course construction. The design and construction teams were very successful, and Shady Oaks became one of the most lavish

club golf courses in the country.

Marty recalled, "I was married at Shady Oaks in June of 1958—it was the first event held there. It wasn't even totally finished. The downstairs wasn't—the upstairs was just finished."

Marvin Leonard had painstakingly built his second masterpiece of a country club. It had cost him about three times what most golf courses cost to build at the time. He would run Shady Oaks for a full year at his own expense before inviting a single member to join. Eventually, the cream of the crop of Fort Worth golfers, including Royal and Ben, would become members at Marvin's Shady Oaks Country Club. It was known for its fine golf course, but also for its wonderfully designed original clubhouse that would become one of Fort Worth's premiere dining and entertainment venues.

Once the layout for the golf course was completed, Ben changed his opinion, and stated, "Anyone who is building a golf course anywhere in the world and doesn't come down to see what has been done at Shady Oaks will be making a big mistake!"

The original ranchland on which Shady Oaks was built, along with the surrounding area Marvin wished to develop, was under the jurisdiction of four separate townships. Marvin developed Ridgmar East in the Fort Worth section, with lots offered at very reasonable prices. Next to Ridgmar East was the small community of Westover Hills, where Marvin developed upscale residences on larger lots. The country club, Shady Oaks, was in Westworth Village, and there was a section in the northwest that was part of the community of White Settlement. These four separate jurisdictions would become a big headache during the development of the neighborhoods.

In 1961, John Maddux would take over the day-to-day management of the development of Ridgmar and the other areas under this four-way jurisdiction. Though Marvin would remain hands on, meeting with Maddux daily, it was John who became responsible for handling the headaches. John Maddux had gone to work for the Leonard brothers at Everybody's when he was sixteen years old. After graduating from Texas Wesleyan College in 1959, he had gone into real estate. Having impressed Marvin with a very interesting sales pitch only a couple of years out of college, Maddux was hired on the spot to work on future Leonard projects. The first phase of Westover had already been finished, but Maddux would oversee the rest of the developments. As stated in *Texas Merchant*, the Victoria and Walter Buenger book on Marvin Leonard's incredible business career, Maddux was invaluable and "revised and finalized lot layouts for five more developmental phases,

and oversaw the installation of streets, sewer systems, and utilities." He was vitally important to Marvin, and they complemented each other very well.

Royal had decided to stay at the Alton Road house, but he would be practically a daily figure at Shady Oaks for the rest of his life. Ben purchased a lot on Canterbury Drive in the new section of Westover Hills. Ben and Valerie had been living on Valley Ridge Road, several blocks away, in an area of Westover Hills that had been developed twelve years before. They built a very roomy brick home on Canterbury that was totally unpretentious. It was decorated in Valerie's favorite colors of blue and white, and there was no reference to golf in the entire house.

JACQUE: *I needlepointed a blue and white pillow of the famous photograph of Uncle Ben's one-iron shot at Merion and gave it to him at Christmas. He really liked it, but Valerie told me, 'We have nothing pertaining to golf in this house.' She took it, and I never saw it again.*

The new home only had one bedroom—purposefully, because Valerie didn't wish to have houseguests. Ben's house was only a short distance from Shady Oaks, his friend Marvin's beautiful new club. The club would become his sanctuary, a home away from home. Ben never truly abandoned Colonial, but Shady Oaks was more private and to his

Marvin Leonard on the eighteenth green at
Shady Oaks Country Club.
Courtesy of Marty Leonard.

liking. Ben was an icon at Colonial and continued to attract a lot of admirers and fans, all wishing to watch him practice or engage him in conversation about golf. He never really liked that, unless it was at his convenience. At Shady Oaks he could hit to shag boys on the Little Nine or on the practice range, and he was very rarely disturbed. Ben had his own regular round table in the men's grill (nineteenth hole), where he would have lunch, usually bean soup with bacon, and share cocktails later in the afternoon with his close group of friends.

Jerre Todd remembers the room at the old clubhouse at Shady Oaks, "The men's grill at Shady Oaks was a medium-sized room. The windows looked out on the eighteenth hole. The round table that Ben, Royal, and their cronies always sat at was located a little left of the center of the room. The table was eight feet in diameter and had a large lazy Susan in the center. Ben always had his chair available, the same chair every day. There was a separate card room where Ben, Marvin Leonard, Earl Baldridge, and the others would play high-stakes gin rummy."

Pucker Barse, a fellow member at Shady Oaks, knew firsthand that Ben was not as aloof and unapproachable as others thought. He said, "I ran into Ben one time in the locker room and said, 'Mr. Hogan I'm having trouble hitting my driver and I practice all the time.' Ben said, 'I know. I watch you while I'm having lunch and it makes me sick to my stomach.' Mr. Hogan gave me a lesson right then, for about twenty minutes. And my driving improved. I loved he took the time to work with me, and I never forgot his lesson."

JACQUE: *Daddy only gambled on the golf course. He never gambled at gin with Ben and his friends, because he was pretty tight with his money when it came to games or investments requiring luck or chance.*

Jerre Todd added, "Yes, but Royal could pretty much always beat those slugs on the golf course, so the chance was reduced greatly."

JACQUE: *Uncle Ben was much more social than folks realize. He was sweet, respectful, funny, and a true gentleman. When not at Shady Oaks, Uncle Ben loved listening to Bing Crosby records, going out to romantic movies, and dancing. When he was delighted by something, he would clap his hands together like a child. He was a dear, dear man.*

Ben and Valerie decided back in the 1950s, as Ben's time on the circuit became shorter and shorter, that they wished to really learn to dance properly. Eddy Deems and his wife had operated the Lavonia Bellah dance studio on Houston Street in downtown Fort Worth since March 1938, and later expanded, opening a Westside studio on Camp Bowie. In 1958, they received two new pupils: Valerie and Ben Hogan.

Eddy recalled, "My wife and I enjoyed teaching the Hogans for a couple of years. Ben approached dancing with the same competitiveness he played golf. He would practice his steps like he would strike ball after ball on the driving range. He became a real good dancer, especially considering the problems he had with his legs. He and Valerie became pretty good at the Lindy Hop, which became known as the jitterbug back when Cab Calloway was performing at the Cotton Club in Harlem. One night Calloway witnessed the young crowd doing the Lindy Hop and remarked, 'They look like a bunch of jitter bugs.'

"Ben was always questioning something during the lessons. One day he asked me, 'Eddy, can you do the same dance step twice?' I said, 'Sure. Of course.' And Ben said, 'Why can't I hit a golf ball the same way twice?' I replied, 'You can't control the ball after you've made impact, but you can control your legs when you dance.' I remember he gave a little laugh, and said, 'Makes sense. Never thought of it that way.'"

Eddy and Lavonia Bellah continued to socialize with the Hogans and their group of friends, including Marvin Leonard and his wife, throughout the 1960s.

Eddy said he really respected Marvin Leonard. "Marvin told me once he sold Colonial to its members because if he died, Obie

Marvin and Obie Leonard in the 1960s.
Courtesy of Marty Leonard.

would bulldoze the course and plant cotton."

Eddy remembers a day he was riding in a golf cart following a friend playing a match at Shady Oaks. "When we got to the fifteenth tee, my friend pointed over at the rough, and there was a corn patch, just off the fairway, about fifteen feet by twenty feet. Marvin had to have his fresh corn. . . . He loved corn on the cob."

Eddy had met his wife Lavonia Bellah when he had taken dance lessons from her. He said he was tired of faking it on the dance floor. They fell in love, were married, and operated the dance business for fifty years. Eddy recently turned ninety-seven years old and still teaches dance at the YMCA in Granbury, Texas.

Present-day photograph of the Hogans' Alton Road house.
Photo by Peter Barbour.

In June of 1973, Earl and Corrine Collins moved in next door to Royal and Margaret on Alton Road. Earl was originally from Corsicana, and Corrine was from up north, near Boston. The two had relocated their family to Fort Worth. It would be a year before they actually met Royal or Margaret, other than to nod or wave.

Earl recalls, "The neighbors had warned us that they were very private and probably wouldn't socialize, as they never had spent much time with any of the other folks on the block."

The first member of the Collins family to actually visit with the Hogans was their son Craig, who was about seven or eight at the time.

Corrine laughed as she related, "We were walking past the Hogans' house on our way home from somewhere, when Mrs. Hogan came out the front door. Craig blurted out something like, 'Hello Mrs. Hogan . . . when can I see your house?' Before I could shush him, Mrs. Hogan lit up, and said, 'How about right now.' Craig dashed for the house, but I went straight home. I thought it would be rude to include myself in my son's curiosity. When he returned, he told me about this great, big, store-sized cooler that had ice cream and Push-Ups, and there were Oreo cookies. And Craig said the house was really neat. It was a couple of years later before I ever saw it."

In 1974, the Collinses hosted a Christmas party, and to their surprise, and that of the neighbors and friends, Royal and Margaret showed up and presented Earl and Corrine with a nice gift.

Corrine recalled, "They stayed for a couple of hours and were very nice. It was a treat for those at the party to meet and visit with Royal and Margaret. Soon after, maybe on New Year's Day 1975, they invited us over to visit and see the house. They showed us around, and I'll never forget the huge, gold, baroque bed in the master bedroom."

The Collins family had a dog named Dusty that was part dachshund, part beagle. Dusty would occasionally roam over to the Hogan's backyard and hunt for squirrels or tree raccoons. There were times that Dusty wouldn't come home, and Earl would hear him bark-ing at a raccoon in the Hogan's backyard.

Earl remembers, "I would run over and have to actually bring the dog home. Dusty was on a mission and wouldn't come when I called, but we had taught him a trick—to play dead. For me to corner him and grab him to take his mind off the raccoon, I would pretend to shoot him and he would fall over dead, and I could grab him and bring him home. I asked Royal once if the dog bark-ing ever bothered him, and he said he never heard anything. But I think he liked Dusty, because Royal loved that the dog would keep the squirrels away. Sometimes, I would get a call from Royal, 'Earl, send Dusty over.' I would let Dusty out and the dog would run toward the Hogans'. Royal would feed Dusty different treats or leftover meats, like pork chops, as a reward for his chores keeping the squirrels out of their yard. But then Dusty also did his business in the Hogan's yard, so I would constantly have to sneak over and shovel the yard to clean up Dusty's refuse. I don't know if they ever saw me do it, but I did it a lot because I was embarrassed our dog would constantly do that."

Earl remembered the time after he had joined Colonial, when he began wondering what Royal thought about the course now that he and Ben spent all of their time out at Shady Oaks. So, one night when they were together, Earl asked Royal what he thought were the best courses to play in Fort Worth.

Earl reported, "He liked Shady Oaks; he said it was really nice. River Crest was a good course, which is totally different—a world of difference there. He liked Mira Vista, and then he paused to think. So, finally I said, 'But Royal, what about Colonial?' And he gave me that look of his, and he said after a long pause, 'Earl, Colonial is a championship course.' And that's all he said. He didn't have to say anything else. The look and short answer said to me, 'You idiot, it's a championship course, what else is there to say?'"

Earl thought Royal was a great person to have next door. He took care of his yard, kept it in pristine condition—and, as Jacque pointed out, if anything broke at her father's house, it was repaired right away. Earl felt he was the perfect neighbor, one who never overstayed his welcome, but always stopped to visit and was always cordial.

Earl never played golf with Royal, but he heard talk that he had more natural ability than Ben did. One day he asked him, "Royal, why didn't you go pro or go on the tour? And he just looked at me and said, 'Well, Earl, one of us had to stay home and go to work.'"

Jacque's son, David Corley, remembered spending time at his grandparents' house. "My grandmother, we called her 'Moms,' was very quiet, very reserved, and was always manicured perfectly. At their house,

Moms had her chair and Pops had his chair. He would play with us kids. We tossed these little throw pillows at one another, but it really unnerved Moms. I think Pops really enjoyed kids. He always had Oreo cookies for us in a big jar in the pantry."

Corrine grew very fond of Margaret, and recalled, "I loved Margaret! She was so elegant. She never went anywhere without her hair perfectly coifed, makeup on and proper, nails done, with color-coordinated attire, like a green dress matched with green jewelry."

JACQUE: *It's like the old expression, it's as if my mother stepped out of a bandbox. Besides her style, Mother had a few other little idiosyncrasies. She loved flowers, yet all of the flowers in our house or garden were plastic. When I was a small girl, I remember if she heard a fire engine, Mother would rustle me out to the car and we would chase the fire truck to the fire. Otherwise, she only drove to the hair salon, the grocery store, and Monnig's department store, all of which were located in the Westcliff Shopping Center. She never drove on a freeway, and she refused to wear a seat belt. I would say "Mother, you have to use a seat belt." And she would tell me, "No, I'm not using it." To satisfy me, she would pull the seat belt across her lap and hold it, but she never buckled it.*

The years of living with Royal had been very hard on Margaret, as it became apparent in the mid 1970s. After Jacque had left for college and her adulthood in the 1950s, Margaret looked after her young son, Royal Dean, without very much assistance from her husband.

Bill West, who lived down the street from the Hogans on Alton Road, was Royal Dean's oldest friend, and he remembers Mrs. Hogan being very protective of her son when he was young.

Bill remembers, "Mrs. Hogan wouldn't allow Royal Dean away from home without some security. Mr. Hogan had a man working for him named Howard Small, and he had a son, Billy, who was a teenager. Mrs. Hogan would send Billy with Royal Dean down to our house to play football or baseball in the backyard. I remember Billy would join in our games—we played sports year round."

When Royal Dean became a teenager, he and his mother yelled at each other a lot. Bill remembers lots of cussing by Royal Dean in those days. It seemed he was always angry with his mother, who had begun to drink a little bit more than moderately. And Royal Dean's relationship with his father deteriorated over arguments like hair length, dress, or activities that Royal didn't approve of.

JACQUE: *Royal Dean became a good junior golfer, but Daddy never encouraged him. And he always was putting him down. After Royal Dean left the house, my mother*

Royal Dean Jr., on the right, with his friend Bill West. Photo courtesy of Bill West.

must have felt all alone, as Daddy would spend more and more time at the store or the club. I think she drank alcohol to get over her depression over the life she was caught up in living. I blame Daddy for my mother becoming an alcoholic.

Margaret Hogan's drinking over the years caught up with her in 1978, when she grew gravely ill with a liver disease. She was taken to the hospital, and suddenly passed away. After she died, Royal wouldn't let anyone touch one thing in the house.

Corrine recalled, "Their maid, Frances, told me he wouldn't let her touch or move anything. Her dresser, her clothes—everything stayed the way she left it the day she went to the hospital. And that's the way it remained until Royal passed away, years later."

Jacque Hogan at SMU.
JHT family collection.

Jacque and her baby brother, Royal Dean Hogan Jr.
JHT family collection.

JACQUE: *I remember going to my mother's funeral with my brother, Royal Dean, and my father. Ben, Valerie, and Mama Hogan were there as well. My mother, as it turned out, had left her half of my parents' estate to my brother and me in trust. Yet I never knew about my mother's will, and didn't see it until eighteen years later, after my father died.*

Jacqueline Hogan had graduated from Paschal High School in 1951. Her teenage years under her father's strict control had been extremely tough, and since her father

had refused to allow her to attend TCU, she made the decision to leave Fort Worth and attend college in Dallas, where she could hope to experience some amount of independence.

Jacqueline had become Jacque her senior year in high school and continued to be known by the nickname when she enrolled at Southern Methodist University, where she joined the Kappa Alpha Theta sorority and made many lifelong friends. Her major at the university was interior design, and she minored in home economics. It was in the

Royal, Aunt Princess, and Royal Dean Jr. at the wedding reception, River Crest Country Club, Fort Worth.
JHT family collection.

The father of the bride and his daughter Jacqueline, in front of St. John's Episcopal Church, Fort Worth.
JHT family collection.

Royal, Margaret, and ring bearer Royal Dean Jr. with Jacqueline, just before the wedding.
JHT family collection.

interior design classes that she met her first husband, David Corley, who was determined not to go into his family mortuary business in his hometown of Corsicana.

Jacque and David were married August 7, 1954, in a splendid ceremony at St. John's Episcopal Church in Fort Worth. Mama Hogan, Aunt Princess and her husband Dr. Howard Ditto, and Ben and Valerie gathered with two hundred fifty other guests to attend the wedding and reception that followed at River Crest Country Club. Jacque's six-year-old brother, Royal Dean Jr., pushed to the front of the bridesmaids and caught his sister's bouquet.

JACQUE: *My bridesmaids weren't happy. He grabbed it and didn't let it go. And then I remember we had asked for the club to provide a couple of bowls of rice by the front door for the guests to ceremoniously throw when we departed. But, I'll never forget, the staff at River Crest cooked the rice. They cooked the rice!*

The couple lived in David's hometown of Corsicana until he started his four-year military commitment. In 1957, David was reassigned to Madrid, and Jacque and he lived on the central square, Plaza Nino Jesus. After David's stint in the Air Force ended in February 1959, they returned to Fort Worth, where David went to work for his father-in-law at the Fort Worth Office Supply Company. Jacque would join him after a year or so, but she never got an office like David's.

At first, David and Jacque rented a two-bedroom house off Bluebonnet Circle that was a nice size for their small family, and in a good neighborhood near TCU. In 1961, Jacque's only son, David Jr., was born in Fort Worth. With the help of David's parents and Jacque's father, the Corleys built a house in the growing subdivision of Overton Park.

David Corley left Hogan Office Supply in 1970 when he realized Royal was never going to pass along the company. David was convinced that his father-in-law was so set in his ways that he couldn't continue to work for him. He found a partner, and the two formed Minton Corley Interior Design.

JACQUE: *David never gave my dad a reason. He just came in one day and said he was leaving and forming an interior design business with Joe Minton. My father always blamed me for David's departure. He was so upset with me that he didn't speak to me, or my children, until I got my divorce from David in 1972.*

After David had left to form Minton Corley, and Jacque was on the outs with her father, she joined her husband's new design firm.

JACQUE: *I was a big part of it at first. I oversaw the inventory. I designed a system to check what Minton Corley had in stock and what was sold and when. It worked really great! But then after a couple of years, David and I got a divorce, and I had to go to work elsewhere.*

Jacque started her own interior design company, but she found there was too much competition to keep her own company afloat. So she went to work at Nettle Creek, an interior design firm that designed and sold bedspreads, pillows, and decorative objects. Over the next decade or so, Jacque would spend her free time looking after her grandmother Mama Hogan and her brother Royal Dean, all the while attempting to satisfy her father's growing demands and needs.

15

"GOLF IS PLAYED WITH WHITE BALLS"

In 1983, Royal turned seventy-four years old and Ben seventy-one, and though both brothers hadn't played tournament golf, amateur or professional, since 1971, they continued to make daily appearances at Shady Oaks. Royal and Ben were very content playing in their regular foursomes and enjoyed matches with each other and their close friends. The men's grill had become a place of refuge for the brothers late each afternoon, as Royal was starting to take it easier as he approached old age, and Ben was avoiding Valerie as much as possible. They loved Shady Oaks, and though they had both slowed down in their later years, they still loved to play golf. And whether on the golf course or at the men's grill, Royal and Ben were still as close as two brothers could be.

For many years up to this time, Royal and Ben had financially supported their mother, while other members of the family had looked after her other needs. Well into her nineties, Mama Hogan had remained active, alert, and for the most part in satisfactory health, except for her progressive hearing loss. She would not always wear her hearing aid, and this greatly frustrated the family. Then, one morning early in 1983, Mama Hogan fell and broke her hip. Unable to walk, she was bedridden, and her health took a turn for the worse. She ended up in the hospital, and after a brief time it was clear she would never completely recover. Clara "Mama" Hogan passed away of natural causes at the age of ninety-three—her greatest legacy the remarkable family she left behind.

Jacque's daughter-in-law, Dayna Corley recalled, "Mama Hogan died soon after David and I got engaged. So I never really knew her, but when I was helping clean out her apartment, she had all of this fabric left over, hundreds of tiny little rolls and all types of material. Under the bed was a box with beautiful, large sections of silk, satin, and exquisite lace. I gave it all to Jacque, and after she knew what I wanted, she made a beautiful wedding dress from Mama Hogan's fabrics for my December wedding later that year."

Clara Williams Hogan had come a long way from her childhood in Comanche, Texas, through a tragic ending to her marriage with Chester Hogan, to working for decades as a seamstress at several stores and raising three children in very difficult times. She still managed to live long enough to witness the tremendous success of Princess, Royal, and Ben. She had been extremely proud of all of her children, and in turn, they all acknowledged what they owed her for their success: the example of her consistent drive for perfection and an incredible work ethic that she demonstrated for the entirety of her life.

Mama Hogan's only grandson, Jacque's brother, Royal Dean Jr., was not so fortunate

Clara "Mama" Hogan, matriarch and rock of the Hogan clan, in the den at the Alton Road house, around 1965.
JHT family collection.

as to enjoy the longevity of the other Hogans. He had a very difficult life, never connecting with his father. From his son's childhood on, Royal was extremely tough on Royal Dean.

JACQUE: *Daddy demanded perfection from my brother, and he expected him to work hard to achieve it, but Royal Dean's true nature was happy-go-lucky. My brother was very outgoing, he loved people, and he loved life. One time, Royal Dean wanted more than*

A new baby arrives—Royal holds Royal Dean Jr.,
with Jacqueline and Margaret Hogan.
JHT family collection.

Royal Dean Hogan Jr., age 10.
Photo by Rhea-Engert.

Royal Dean Hogan Jr., Paschal High School
yearbook photograph.
Photo by Rhea-Engert.

anything to buy a really old car and restore it, When he approached Daddy for the money, Daddy told him, "That's stupid, you can't do that." Daddy was really hard on him most of the time.

Royal Dean had been a very good young golfer, winning a junior tournament at Colonial when he was fifteen years old. Ironically, his father never encouraged him at golf, never helped him, and habitually berated him about one thing or another. Extremely troubled and confused, Royal Dean dropped out of high school and turned to drinking and drugs.

JACQUE: *Finally he had enough of his relationship with my father and moved to Aspen. Unfortunately, he fell in with the wrong crowd, began to drink more and more, and*

Alternative lifestyles in the Rockies—Bill West visits his old friend Royal Dean Jr. (wearing white sunglasses), in Aspen, Colorado.
Courtesy of Bill West.

was experimenting with all types of drugs. He would call me at two o'clock in the morning and he always sounded intoxicated. I would say, "You need to get some help to stop what you're doing." He surprised me by leaving Aspen after some number of years and returning to Fort Worth. He fell into a very serious relationship with a registered nurse named Susan, and they moved in together in an apartment on El Campo, where I visited them many times. Royal Dean seemed to be in a good place during this time. Susan was accepted at a nursing school in Galveston to advance her education in her field, and Royal Dean moved down to the Gulf Coast with her. Within a few months, he called, all upset, and said that Susan had had all she could take of his drinking and had left him. He asked me if I could come to Galveston and help him. I told him I couldn't leave, I had responsibilities, but if he could come to Fort Worth, I would find him an alcohol rehabilitation center.

Royal Dean returned to Fort Worth, and Jacque found a credible alcohol and drug treatment center in Wichita Falls. She called her dad and said Royal Dean was willing to go get some help, but that it wasn't going to be cheap. At first Royal, totally frustrated with his son, wanted to wash his hands of the matter altogether and was reluctant to help. Jacque insisted that it was Royal Sr.'s responsibility to help his son, and he had to pay for the treatment. Finally, Royal acquiesced, and Royal Dean Jr. headed for Wichita Falls.

JACQUE: *In a short time, Royal Dean really cleaned up his act. I went up there for weekly meetings for months. I would visit with him and his counselors. I remember after several months, he was really starting to look good again. The advice we kept getting from the clinic was that Royal Dean should not return to Fort Worth. They told him he could pick anywhere in the whole wide world to start over, but not to return to Fort Worth. They feared he would be tempted to return to his old 'group of friends' and again be under the negative influence of his father.*

But when it was time to be released, Royal

Dean thought he would be fine in Fort Worth, telling Jacque "It is my home." Within two months, as the clinic predicted, he was running with the same bunch of ne'er-do-wells from his alcoholic past.

JACQUE: *I don't think it was my brother's fault. He had a disease. Daddy, like many others, felt that alcoholism was a weakness of will, but it's not—it's a disease. Some people are lucky and they recover, but some never do.*

Unfortunately, Royal Dean was right back where he was before his treatment. He didn't have to worry about money, as his father had set him and Jacque up some years before, transferring a percentage of some of his interests in oil, and these monthly royalties provided plenty of funds for Royal Dean's lifestyle. It had become evident to his sister that he supported some of his drinking buddies from his good fortune as well.

JACQUE: *My daddy set it up so that Royal Dean and I could get income from a percentage of his royalties, but I was in my thirties. My brother was a teenager, and when he turned twenty-one, Daddy set it up for him to receive a trust fund that held a considerable amount of cash. My brother never had to work a day in his life. I really fault my father for giving him easy access to so much money, when he was so tough on him in every other way. Maybe he thought it would*

compensate for that, but I think the financial independence at such an early age really enabled a path to his nightmarish lifestyle.

Royal Dean's oldest friend, Bill West, agrees, "Back in the 1970s, I was working five days a week, earning about $8,000 to $9,000 a year. Royal Dean didn't have a job, but he had that trust with Moncrief Oil company royalties that paid him about $23,000 a year. That was a lot of money for a twenty-year-old to have without working for it. I used to say to him, 'Royal Dean, you need to get a job.' He would say, 'What am I going to do? Besides, I don't need to work.'"

One day Royal Dean, who had been drinking, received a royalty check in the mail that he felt he had to deposit. Royal Dean walked out and got into his Jeep. He started it up and drove it toward the exit to the apartment parking lot in Ridgmar. Coming down a hill, the Jeep spun out of control and crashed into a fence. Royal Dean was not hurt, but he just left the car and walked back up to his apartment. When the manager dropped by to tell him he had to move the car, Royal Dean said he would get to it later.

JACQUE: *The manager called the police. My brother had a great fear of policemen. I don't know why—maybe because he was paranoid about going to jail. Anyway, a policeman knocked at his door and said he was going to assist him returning his crashed Jeep* back to a legitimate parking space. The policeman told me later he didn't think Royal Dean was too inebriated, or he would never have asked him to move his car.

The name of Royal Dean's apartment complex was the Steppes. There were various units located on several hills, and there were concrete steps running up and down throughout the complex. To get to where his car was, he and the policeman had to go down this short flight of steps. Somehow, Royal Dean tripped and fell at the very top of the concrete stairs. The policeman couldn't stop him as he tumbled down to the bottom of the eight steps, where he lay unconscious. Besides other injuries, Royal Dean had suffered a severe concussion. The paramedics were called and they rushed him to the emergency room, but he never regained consciousness. The doctors tried everything to revive him, but it was hopeless. Royal Dean Hogan Jr. died the next morning. It was 1986, and Royal Dean was thirty-eight years old.

JACQUE: *After Royal Dean's funeral, Daddy told me to go over to his apartment in Ridgmar and box up everything and bring it to the Alton Road house. When I got to the Steppes, I found that someone who obviously knew Royal Dean had broken in and stolen his very expensive bicycle and no telling what else. The place had been turned upside down. When I told my father about the break-in, he* blamed me for not having attended to it earlier. He suddenly went into a rage and started screaming at me. I was so fed up with him and so disgusted that I said in a calm, deliberate tone of voice, "You killed my mother, you killed my brother . . . but you will never kill me."

Her brother's tragic death severely affected Jacque; she had tried for so many years to provide the support and encouragement he never seemed to get from their father. However disappointed she was in the way their father treated his son, Jacque would spend the next several years taking care of Royal Sr.

The year after Royal Dean passed away, his father was diagnosed with colon cancer. As soon as the prognosis was delivered, Royal had surgery in Fort Worth. For several months, Jacque would drive her father to Dallas for chemotherapy and radiation treatments. The cancer in his colon eventually went into remission, but despite that hopeful turn, the cancer metastasized and moved into his lungs, requiring a second surgery. Jacque's son David had done his residency at Baylor Hospital in Dallas, and suggested to his grandfather that he should have his next surgical procedure done there. The operation and treatments were successful, and Royal was once again cancer free by the end of 1990.

For several years, Royal had been experiencing problems with his vision. Don Bassham recalled that in the 1980s, Royal would strain to read, and had to use a magnifying glass to see the invoices and sign the checks.

Don recalled, "He had this magnifying contraption sitting on top of a credenza right behind his desk. He had eye problems for a while, but he was like everybody else; he tried to fake it."

In the late 1980s, however, Royal developed cataracts, and the condition required surgery. After recovering from the surgery he continued to have trouble with his vision, and blamed the surgeon who had done the operation. His vision was getting worse, and Jacque was concerned about his driving, but he refused to stop. Jacque took him to another doctor, who diagnosed the real cause of his increasing blindness: macular degeneration. That deteriorating condition affected the back of his retina, causing a black "hole" in the center of Royal's vision, as if someone were holding a fist in front of his eyes. He could not focus on anything directly in front of him, yet he was still able to see fairly clearly in his periphery. Jacque had already arranged for the physician to talk to Royal about his stubborn insistence upon driving. After the diagnosis was discussed, the doctor turned to Royal and said, "Listen Mr. Hogan, it is not safe for you to drive. You must never drive again, for if you have a wreck and

Royal Hogan in his later years in the men's grill at Shady Oaks Country Club.
JHT family collection.

maim or kill somebody, I'll have to tell them that I told you under no circumstances were you to drive. And if that happens, I fear you might be sued for everything you have."

That was all it took. Royal handed the keys over to his daughter, and Jacque began to drive him to dinner, to the various doctors, to the store, to the country club, and to any other places he needed to go. She even went back to work for him at Hogan Office Supply Company. Expected to be on call, Jacque no longer had a life of her own. She would pick up her father every morning, drive him to the store, drive him to dinner after work, then drive him back home. She became his 24/7 caregiver.

At the store, she tried to make the most of her time by attempting to modernize the offices. For example, Royal was still renting dial-up phones. Jacque pointed out to her father that no one rented telephones anymore, and no one used a dial phone.

JACQUE: *If you wanted to place an order, you had to push buttons to finish the process, and I couldn't do that. I had to go home and place an order on my "modern" phone, and then go back to work. It was a real waste of time, and finally I convinced Daddy to change the phone system, but it was a struggle.*

After Jacque returned to work for her father, she also realized the copy machine at Hogan Office Supply was from the dark ages. She replaced it and was going to have it thrown out, but her father said to put it up for sale at the front of the store. "Daddy, nobody will buy it. It's a relic." But, to her surprise, somebody purchased the ancient machine.

JACQUE: *I couldn't believe somebody bought it! And, the store also had white legal pads that had turned yellow. There was glue that had turned solid. And these were on his shelves. I said, "Daddy, these things should be thrown out." Because his vision was more and more impaired, he really couldn't inspect the product, so he would say, "They're okay, just leave them there, we're going to sell them." He wouldn't throw anything away.*

Because of his macular degeneration, Roy-al had to give up golf, which had been his passionate hobby for most of his life. One day his grandson David and David's wife Dayna took him to his new favorite restaurant, Olive Garden, where he loved the breadsticks and their big salads. Royal was talking about the art of golf, figuring the wind speeds and elevation to the greens. All the knowledge he had accumulated about the game fascinated David and Dayna.

Royal lamented, "I can't see the ball, even if I hit it properly. I never know where my ball is going."

Dayna, trying to help, said, "You know Pops, they make these new balls. I've seen them. They are fluorescent orange, and maybe you could see them better."

Royal gave her a look of consternation and said, "Golf is played with white balls."

David and Dayna looked at each other and sort of shrugged their shoulders. As Dayna later recalled, "That was it. We're done. Golf is played with white balls. End of discussion."

No longer able to play golf, Royal spent his weekends with football or golf on the television, mostly listening, since he couldn't focus on the images. Or when the team was playing, he would tune his radio to the TCU football games. He became a creature of habit when it came to going out to lunch or dinner, so if they didn't eat at the Olive Garden, or

Shady Oaks, or Joe T.'s, he would go to the Lone Star Oyster Bar on Bryant Irvin Road, where he loved the fried shrimp. Jacque, David, and Dayna tried to take him to different places like Chinese restaurants or something brand new, but he never liked them.

David recalled, "When we would take him for dinner, Pops would always demand to pay for the meal, and then he would leave a tip of only about five percent. He really didn't believe in tipping. As we were leaving, Dayna or I would linger behind and add some money to bring the tip up to a proper percentage.

JACQUE: *Daddy and Uncle Ben, for most of their lives, had little quirks when it came to dining out. When they sat at a table, both of them would pick up the fork, knife, and spoon, and carefully clean them with their napkins. It was their little ritual. If they were in a good steak restaurant, they always asked for steak sauce. Sometimes, the chef would come out and say, "These are perfect the way they are." Daddy would say, "It might be perfect for you, and it'll be perfect for me when I get some steak sauce." And, like me, Daddy always had to have his steaks well done, and so did Uncle Ben.*

Ben began to slow down in the late 1980s. In fact, his protégé, Kris Tschetter, wrote a book entitled *Mr. Hogan, The Man I Knew*. In it, she wrote that she played with her mentor in what would be Ben's last round of golf, on August 28, 1986. Ben joined Kris and two college golf teammates, Kirsten Larson and Elle Gibson, and they played the back nine at Shady Oaks. Ben hadn't played a round of golf in several years, but still managed to shoot an even par that hot summer day in Fort Worth. After this round with Kris and the others, Ben continued to hit practice balls, but never played another round of golf.

Kris wrote that her family had moved to Fort Worth when she was a teenager, and they joined Shady Oaks. As a freshman member of the TCU golf team, she spent a lot of time hitting practice balls on the range, and this attracted Ben's attention. Kris had learned early on not to bother him. But she was friendly with all of the other members, so one day she said hello to Mr. Hogan. That started a conversation that evolved into a mentor/protégé relationship that lasted the rest of Ben's life.

JACQUE: *Uncle Ben spent a lot of time coaching Kris. They were very close and had a great relationship. I think Valerie was a little bit jealous.*

Ray Coleman, Ben's long-time sales manager at the Hogan Company, recalls, "One day, Mr. Hogan went to a jewelry store and had them design a silver medallion with a little diamond on it. He directed that the medallions would be presented to any golfer who lettered on the women's golf team at TCU. He did this anonymously—no one ever knew

Buster waits for Ben for another round of golf.
Courtesy of Shady Oaks Country Club and Mike Wright.

Mr. Hogan paid for the medallions. This showed a generous side of Mr. Hogan that most people aren't aware of. Some of the people who worked at the Hogan Company felt it was because of his closeness to Kris Tschetter that Mr. Hogan did it."

When Mike Wright, the current head pro at Shady Oaks Country Club, arrived at his first day of work in 1984, he opened the door to the pro shop and was surprised that he had to step over two sleeping dogs.

Mike recalled, "That was unusual, but when I learned the story of the dogs and the importance of these pets to Mr. Hogan, Mr.

Moncrief, and all of the club members, it all made sense to me."

During the late 1970s, Buster, a small salt and pepper colored Schnauzer, started showing up at Shady Oaks. The actual home of his owners was across the street from the club, but the dog decided to adopt the contoured fairways of the golf course as his day camp and the clubhouse as his daily lunch diner. The members started to take a liking to Buster, especially Ben and Tex, who would feed him and take him in their carts on a round of golf.

One day, on his trek back to his house from Shady Oaks, a car ran over Buster. His back legs were severely injured and he was unable to walk. His owners made a home for Buster in their garage while they hoped for him to recover. The members of Shady Oaks were beside themselves missing their canine ambassador, and would drop by whenever they could to share treats with their injured companion. Over the next few weeks, the owners of Buster became so overwhelmed by the members of Fort Worth high society that visited their dog every day that they set up a guest book for the movers and shakers to sign—the "Buster Guest Book".

After several weeks, incredibly, Buster picked himself up and crawled across the street, dragging himself to the clubhouse at Shady Oaks. Ben was excited to see him and lifted him into his cart for a round of golf. Buster was back home.

Mike related, "The family who owned Buster was about to move away from Fort Worth. They contacted Tex Moncrief, who was the president of the club at the time, and told him that they felt Buster belonged to Shady Oaks, and they would feel horrible about taking him away from the real home he loved. Tex assured the family he would take care of Buster, and from that day on, Ben or Tex made sure the dog had food and veterinarian services. For many years after, Ben looked after Buster as if he had always been his own."

A couple of years later, another dog, a beautiful Border Collie that the club members named Max, showed up out of nowhere. As much as they tried, the members at Shady Oaks couldn't find the owners, so they adopted Max as a new member of the club. A painting of Max and Ben still adorns the wall of the dining room at Shady Oaks today.

Mike recalled, "Buster and Max would roam throughout the clubhouse, even in the dining room while the members were eating lunch or dinner. It was amazing—the dogs had the run of the club and no one complained. At night, I was told that Buster would sleep in Ben's chair at the round table in the men's grill, but I think that story might be a part of the Shady Oaks mythology."

This painting of Ben Hogan and the other beloved, adopted dog at Shady Oaks, the beautiful Border Collie Max, hung in the entryway to the dining room at the old clubhouse. Courtesy of Shady Oaks Country Club and Mike Wright.

After Buster died, the club had a ceremony and placed a granite plaque for their beloved pet near the putting green. One night, soon after Buster had been honored with the me-

The memorial marker for Buster that sits beside
the putting green at Shady Oaks.
Photo by Jacque Towery

morial, Mr. and Mrs. Hogan showed up at
the club, and Valerie asked Mike if Ben could
visit the site where Buster was buried.

"It was a very cold night, and Mr. Hogan
was wearing an overcoat," Mike recalled. "I
remember his wife and I stopped at the door
as Mr. Hogan walked out to where the stone
honored Buster. He removed his hat and
placed it over his heart. Then, he got down
on his knees, looked up, pressed his fingers
to his lips and then touched them to Buster's
plaque. It was a very tender moment to witness. One that I will never forget."

Following the concept Ben brought to
the Masters, Colonial Country Club started
a tradition of hosting a Champions Dinner,
held each year on the Wednesday before the
tournament started. One of the long-time

members of the tournament committee, Scott
Corpening, recalled the last time Ben and
Valerie attended a Champions Dinner. It was
in 1990, and when Ben and Valerie arrived at
Colonial, Scott showed them into the manager's office so they could have some privacy
before "meeting the masses" at the dinner.
Scott set up a small bar in the manager's office and asked the Hogans if they would like
a soda, a glass of wine, or water.

Valerie replied, "We will take two ice waters."

Ben said, "I'd like a white wine."

Scott froze and looked at Valerie, who
looked over at her husband, and said, "Ben,
they're going to have wine at dinner, and
you've been out at Shady Oaks having your
cocktails, so I think water will do just fine."

Ben turned to her and said, "You can have
a glass of water, but I'm getting a glass of
wine."

Scott remembers, "A little reluctantly, I
brought a glass of wine and a glass of water,
and placed the glasses between them. Valerie
reached out and slid the glass of wine in front
of her, but then Ben reached over and slid it
back in front of him. This happened several
times, before suddenly Lanny Wadkins came
in and interrupted them. He paid his respects
to Ben, who by that point had a very firm
grip on his glass of wine."

After Lanny, Ben and Julie Crenshaw arrived and greeted Valerie and Ben. They sat down for a short visit. Fuzzy Zoeller then appeared with a cigarette and a vodka tonic and greeted the Hogans with his folksy manner, lightening the tension and mood in the room.

Scott recalls what happened next. "After a while, the group was ready to go into the dining room. Julie and my wife escorted Valerie toward the lobby, while Ben Crenshaw and I were walking with Mr. Hogan. We reached the Hogan Room, the old, smaller version just off the lobby, and the two Bens walked into the room to take a look. I stayed at the door and watched as these two great golfers looked over the various trophies, rings, and medals that Mr. Hogan had won over his astonishing career. As they were leaving the room, Mr. Hogan cleared his throat, and pointed back at the room, and asked Ben, 'Are all of these mine?' To which Crenshaw replied, 'Yes sir, Mr. Hogan. Yes they are.' Mr. Hogan gave a sly smile and said, 'I really must have been something.' I began to tear up when Ben Crenshaw, who was also choking back tears, said, 'Mr. Hogan, you were a lot more than something.' This was the first sign I ever saw of the dementia that would plague Mr. Hogan for the years to come."

Jacque started to notice it when she took Ben and Valerie to dinner at Shady Oaks, and various people would stop by the table to visit and pay their respects to her uncle. After

Ben Hogan at 80.
JHT family collection.

they left, Ben would turn to Valerie or Jacque and ask, "Who was that?"

JACQUE: *Uncle Ben was as sweet as ever, but it was sad to see him in his declining years. Yet no matter what, he still had a sense of humor. When the weather was nice, I would take them to Shady Oaks, and we would park the car on the lower level and walk through the tunnel to an entrance to the dining room. If it was raining, I would drive up to the main level porte cochère where Uncle Ben would tell me to leave the car. We would enter the lobby and descend the stairs to the lower level. At the bottom of the stairs, Uncle Ben would stop and smile, saying, "They're all still here," referring to the number of steps. He would do this every time, and it always made me smile.*

Ben Hogan holds the US Open trophy along with the five medallions
he won at the event during his career. (Four US Open victories and one
Hale America Open championship in 1942).
JHT family collection.

One night, Jacque was at dinner at Shady Oaks with Ben and Valerie. Her uncle told Jacque that with the proper coaching and lots of practice, he could get her in golfing shape to play on the LPGA tour. He stood up and demonstrated the proper grip, stance and address to the ball. He took several imaginary swings at a golf ball all the while telling Jacque a little bit of the secret he had discovered so many years before.

JACQUE: *I'm sure the rest of the people in the dining room were getting a big kick out of watching Ben Hogan demonstrate the proper golf mechanics. Well, everyone except Valerie, who after a short while grabbed Ben's arm and said, "Sit down, Ben, you're embarrassing me."*

Jacque continued to look after her father, and occasionally she would take Ben and Valerie out for dinner with her father and Sarah. Jacque had adjusted to her servitude to Royal, and she still loved to spend time with her Uncle Ben. Then in 1991, Jacque attended the fortieth year reunion of her Paschal High School class, where she ran into an old classmate, Robert Towery.

ROBERT: *When Jacque and I met again at our fortieth high school reunion, we renewed our friendship. I was living in Austin, and my marriage was falling apart. Long-time friends were trying to get me to move back to Fort Worth, and I visited several times. Jacque and*

Valerie and Ben Hogan with Jacque, outside of Shady Oaks Country Club. JHT family collection.

I saw each other with other friends, and our friendship developed into a companionship, and then something more. Both of us had been married and weren't sure we wanted to take that step again. But the more we were with each other, the more we felt there was a future for us together. We decided to spend a few days away from our usual environments, and we chose to meet in San Antonio.

Jacque told her father that she would be

gone for a few days and that she had arranged for someone to drive for him while she was away. Royal exploded. He threw a fit, slamming doors, yelling, finally saying that if she did this, he would fire her. But Jacque was strong minded as well, and she believed the trip was very important.

JACQUE: *I remember asking my father, "Now let me get this straight. If I leave, I'm fired?" And he said, "That's right." I looked at him with a bit of disgust, and quietly said, "Well, then, goodbye."*

Jacque made the decision to go, but there were a few things she needed to do before she left town. Since she was driving him everywhere, Royal had purchased a new Cadillac for Jacque, but he purchased it in the name of the Hogan Office Supply Company. Jacque held a power-of-attorney to act for her father, and she took steps to transfer title to the car from the company to her individually. She knew that if she didn't do this, Royal might send the police looking for her car to take it away from her. Since her teenage years, if she did something that displeased her father, he had always taken away her car.

Before Jacque left to meet Robert in San Antonio, she arranged for a Hogan Office Supply employee, James Tucker, who had replaced Howard Small, to take over the task of driving her father. Jacque figured that her father would probably never forgive her.

Nevertheless, she believed it would be worth trying to reconcile when she returned from San Antonio, and she hoped he would once again accept her aid and attention.

JACQUE: *That didn't happen. When I returned, Daddy refused to see me, and he didn't talk to me again until he was at the very end of his life. It's a shame, but he wouldn't meet or even speak with Robert. And Daddy would have benefited from knowing this nice man. After all, he had come such a long way from that boy my father treated so badly the day at Glen Garden when Robert refused to go into the lake to retrieve Daddy's driver.*

ROBERT: *I never got to know Royal Hogan personally. I had one encounter with him when I caddied at Glen Garden Golf and Country Club, but I never met him when Jacque and I were in high school. By the time Jacque and I got married, he was estranged from his daughter, and we never shook hands or talked. In so many ways, Royal was an accomplished and honorable individual, and I do not intend to downgrade his success. However, he had a controlling nature that seldom showed, but it had some devastating effects on Margaret, Royal Dean Jr., and Jacque.*

16

THE FINAL YEARS

Jacque and her father became estranged in the summer of 1991. Royal had severed all contact with his daughter, so that her previous duties and responsibilities in caring for him were a thing of the past. Jacque called her father on his birthday, on Father's Day, on other holidays, and every once in a while just to check on how he was doing. The calls were pretty lopsided, as Royal's responses to her seldom amounted to more than a "yes" or "no" to her inquiries about his recent activities or his present condition and health. As much as she tried to engage him with many phone calls, he would not cooperate. She only saw him once over the next five years, and that occurred on February 16, 1995.

JACQUE: *It was my father's birthday, and I had given him a call early in the day, but he was not very friendly and mostly unresponsive. That night, Robert and I went to the Olive Garden on Hulen to have dinner, and we ran into my father. He was with David and Dayna. I was just as surprised to see him as he was to see me, but I could tell my daddy was utterly displeased with the encounter. I later learned he got really mad at David and Dayna because he thought they had actually planned a "chance" meeting with me as a birthday surprise.*

Jacque and her father wouldn't see each other again until December 1996, when Royal was in Harris Hospital near the end of his life. Since the 1991 falling out with

Ben Hogan greets the golfers at the first tee at the 1992 Southwestern Bell Colonial Invitational. LEFT TO RIGHT: patrol officer Charlie Cripliver, Ben Hogan, Wally Schmuck, and behind them two other Colonial members, Roland Harper and Clark Martin
Courtesy of Wally Schmuck.

her father, Jacque had turned her attention to looking after Valerie and her Uncle Ben. Three times a week, she would pick them up and drive them to Shady Oaks for dinner. In spite of the fact that Ben was starting to lose his memory by incremental degrees, he was

still very pleasant to be around, and Jacque looked forward to her time with him.

During the late 1980s and early 1990s, Dennis Roberson, the Colonial tournament manager, remembers Valerie would call and say that she and Ben wanted to come out and watch some of the golf. He recalled, "We would set a day, and arrange for security. One year, or a couple maybe, we asked Bank One if they would host Ben and Valerie in their sixteenth hole corporate box. Of course, we asked them to make sure no one bothered Mr. Hogan. They accommodated us, and I think the Hogans really enjoyed their time watching the tournament from a very comfortable vantage point."

One day in early May of 1992, Jacque received a call from Wally Schmuck, the head of the Colonial tournament committee, who asked her if she could persuade Ben and Valerie to make an appearance at the Southwestern Bell sponsored Colonial tournament coming up in the next couple of weeks.

JACQUE: *I said okay, but I didn't promise anything. I called Valerie and asked if we could take Ben out to meet some of the golfers. I was surprised: she said, "Okay." But I think she was sorry the minute she agreed.*

On Friday, May 22, 1992, Jacque and Robert drove over to the Canterbury house to pick up Ben and Valerie. Jacque was driving, and Ben sat in the front seat as he always did.

With Valerie and Robert in the rear, Jacque drove the car to the valet station in front of the four huge white columns at the entrance to the red-bricked Colonial clubhouse.

Scott Corpening, another member of the committee, recalls, "We were concerned about a mob scene, so instead of taking Ben through the clubhouse and out to the golf course where all of the galleries were passing here and there, we immediately loaded him into a golf cart. Charlie Cripliver, a very respected local policeman who was well known at Colonial, was standing on the back of the cart to beef up security. Wally drove Mr. Hogan out onto the street and down to a little-known gate where they entered the course at the back of the first tee."

Behind the championship tee, the committee had set up a table with chairs for Mr. Hogan. Ben produced a little piece of paper on which he had written the names of players he wanted to watch. He was still fascinated with the precision of a perfect takeaway, dead center contact, and flowing follow-through. He had seen the present golfers on TV, and his list represented those whose swings he admired.

Scott recalled, "Some of the golfers would walk over and whisper to me, 'Is that really Mr. Hogan?' All of them were very impressed and reverent in his presence."

The players would come over to the table to pick up their scorecards, pencils, and tees, and every one of the professionals paid their respects to the legendary golfer sitting at the table. Some of them shook Ben's hand and had a short visit, while others, totally surprised by his presence, would ask him to sign their hat, glove, or any piece of paper they could lay their hands on.

Ben told Wally Schmuck and Scott Corpening that he wanted to see Brian Claar tee off. This surprised them, as Brian was a journeyman golfer and not really in contention. They figured since Brian was a slight gentleman like Ben, that the Wee Ice Man had taken a particular interest in his swing.

Scott recalled, "Brian showed up at the table, picked up his scorecard and a pencil, and walked toward the tee box. I approached Brian and said, 'Mr. Hogan would like to meet you.' Brian looked around and said, 'Where is he?' I said, 'He's sitting at that table where you just were.' Brian panicked because he had been that close to him and hadn't acknowledged him. I brought him over and introduced him to Mr. Hogan, and I think Brian was speechless."

After watching Brian tee off, Ben was excited to meet Davis Love III, who he thought had an excellent swing for a man with a taller, more slender frame. The two shook hands, and Davis was obviously pleased to talk with Ben Hogan.

Rita Eatherly, Charles Cripliver, Ben Hogan,
and Wally Schmuck observe golfers on the
fifth hole during Colonial's 1992 NIT.
Courtesy of Wally Schmuck.

After watching several pairs of golfers drive their first shots down the 565-yard par-five opening hole, Ben asked Wally if they could go out on the course and see some play on holes three, four, and five. Driving just inside the ropes and with the policeman still on the back of the cart, Wally drove Ben around the "horrible horseshoe." When a golfer was nearby, he would come over to the cart and shake hands with the legend.

Scott remembered, "Mr. Hogan was told there were some reserved seats for him, Valerie, Jacque, and Robert in the Bank One skybox behind the sixteenth green, so he could watch the golfers play the par three. He said that would be perfect."

As the cart was returning to the first tee, Ben told Wally he really wished to meet Greg Norman. They sent out word and found Greg on the practice range. Within five minutes the Great White Shark was shaking hands with Ben behind the first tee. They had a quiet conversation, and then Greg accompanied the entourage into the clubhouse. While the committee members looked on, the two number-one golfers from separate eras posed for a photograph together in front of the Hogan trophy room.

While her Uncle Ben had been out on the course, the committee officials had shown Jacque, Robert, and Valerie into the club's ballroom. The corporate sponsor offered

Ben Hogan and Greg Norman pose for a photograph during the 1992 Southwestern Bell Colonial, in the old Hogan room off the main entrance to the clubhouse.
Courtesy of Wally Schmuck.

them a drink, and then they walked over to the sixteenth green and waited by the stairs to the skybox for Ben to arrive as scheduled.

JACQUE: *I remember Valerie was very up-tight. I think she was mad that they had whisked Uncle Ben away, and she had lost her control of the situation. When Uncle Ben arrived where we were waiting behind the sixteenth green, we helped him up the steps at the back of the skybox. It was very hard for him to walk. Then we had to go down a lot of steps to the front row and over to the far right side where Uncle Ben wanted to sit.*

Jacque Towery with Elizabeth Hudson.
Photo by Peter Barbour.

He had just arrived at his seat and was about to sit down when Valerie said, "We're going." I was stunned and said, "Valerie, Uncle Ben just got here. Let him rest." But she wouldn't even let him sit down and repeated very loudly, "We're GOING!" And with that, we had to leave. It was a shame, because it was Uncle Ben's last time at a tournament, and he only wanted to watch some of the pros play the par-three sixteenth, but she fixed that.

Scott Corpening reflected, "I think Mr. Hogan had really enjoyed meeting and greeting the various pros that day. Mr. Hogan

couldn't have been any nicer. He seemed to be very shy, introverted, but when you got to know him, he was very conversational. Over the years, when our new Champion Choices (two young pros picked for their first time to play in the tournament) came out to the Champions Dinner, they would take a picture with Mr. Hogan, and all of them would ask me if they could get an autographed copy. I would call Doxie Williams or Pat Martin at the factory and set up an appointment to see Mr. Hogan. I would take out the eight-by-tens and go into Ben's office, and he took his time with every autograph. He would meticulously sign each, because he wanted his signature to look right. We would visit, talk about Colonial's shape, the tournament, or Shady Oaks, and he couldn't have been more cordial and engaging during those talks."

After that 1992 appearance at Colonial, Valerie became more and more protective of Ben being seen in public. She was also getting to the point where she didn't want anyone to bother him at home. Elizabeth Hudson, who had worked for Ben and Valerie since 1983, saw a change come over Valerie during the years she was employed at the Canterbury house. Elizabeth arrived every weekday morning, and at first, she would do whatever was needed to help Gladys, the Hogans' housekeeper of thirty years, or Willa May, the Hogans' cook. Occasionally, she spent time driving Mr. Hogan to and from Shady Oaks. Once a year, she would drop by Colonial and polish the trophies in the Hogan Room a couple of weeks before the Invitational tournament, and if Mrs. Hogan needed her on the weekends, she was on call to help out.

Elizabeth commented, "I'd go over there on weekends, and that house would be so dark. She would have all the curtains closed, and no lights were on. It was just dark. I always tried to open the curtains. But Mrs. Hogan would say, 'Leave the curtains closed.' Oh my, I thought, who wanted to stay in a dark house!"

ROBERT: *If there was a negative influence in Ben's life, Jacque believes—and I concur—it was Valerie . . . not the death of his father. The one thing in Ben's life that she could not control, or even influence, was golf. Perhaps this was another motivation for Ben to spend so much time practicing and playing golf and sitting around the club . . . [and it] also prompted him to spend extended periods of time, during three separate years, residing at the Western Hills Hotel on Camp Bowie Boulevard, an establishment in which Ben owned a financial interest.*

Starting around 1992, Elizabeth started to see more differences at the Hogan home. It seemed that Valerie was afraid of anyone seeing evidence of Ben's dementia, and this controlled her every action. Ben hadn't really changed, as he would still get up every morning, take his long bath, and then dress himself in pants, dress shirt, coat, and tie. The end result was always the same. Ben was impeccably attired to the end.

Elizabeth remembered, "Mr. Hogan loved to watch golf on the TV, but that was only on the weekends. Mrs. Hogan made him watch soap operas during the week. Can you imagine, a man like Ben Hogan having to watch soap operas? And people from Fort Worth, or celebrities like Arnold Palmer or Tiger Woods, would call him at the house, and she wouldn't let them talk to him. One day she came up to me and said, 'I got it fixed, Elizabeth.' And, I said, 'What did you do?' And she answered, 'I fixed it so when they come here [to Fort Worth], they can't call me—they have to call the lawyer, who knows to tell them no.' Mrs. Hogan got to the point she wouldn't let anyone see him, except the other Mr. Hogan or Mr. Moncrief. They came by all the time, because she couldn't stop them from dropping in."

While having dinner with her uncle at Shady Oaks, Jacque noticed that Ben would constantly scratch his arms and complain about the itchiness of his skin. Jacque told him he should use a lotion to help moisturize his skin, and promised that this would really help him. Jacque told Ben that she would bring some lotion by his house to see if it would alleviate his condition, and she did that on several occasions.

JACQUE: *I would ask him about it the next time I saw him. "How did that lotion work?" He would look at me like, "What lotion?" And Valerie would say, "Oh, it didn't work." I wondered if she just threw it away.*

Elizabeth added, "She probably did. I never saw any lotion. And I think he was itching because she made him drink all of that orange juice. She claimed that was going to keep him alive. Keep him healthy. She made him drink a lot of it. And, it had to be fresh squeezed every day. Every day. She made him drink that and he just kept itching and itching. Bless his heart. He was the nicest, sweetest man; he was a good, good person. But I remember Mrs. Hogan would say to Mr. Hogan, 'You've always been too good to people. You can't be all things to all people, you just can't do that.' That's what she told him."

Ben's doctor had been Dr. Jim Murphy ever since his brother-in-law, Dr. Howard Ditto, died in 1970. Dr. Murphy was a member at Shady Oaks and River Crest. He always loved the game of golf and was very reverent toward Ben. During the 1970s and 1980s, Valerie's sister, Sarah, and her husband, Gordon Harriman, had become very close to the Murphys. The couple would socialize among the same circle of friends, including the Tex Moncriefs, the Fred Dickeys, the Jimmy Rileys, and of course, Valerie and Ben. Dr. Murphy laughed as he said, "You know, Jimmy Riley was the only one I knew who called Ben, 'Henny Bogan.' Our group was pretty close, since we all got along with each other so well. Gordon Harriman and I played a lot of golf, and I became very close to him and Sarah. Sarah played golf pretty regularly, with a group called 'The Shady Ladies,' and she was a very good player. Ben encouraged her a lot. She was just a superior gal. She had a lot more personality than her sister, Valerie; in fact, they were almost opposite personalities, with Sarah being a lot more outgoing. When Gordon died from a tumor in his lung, Sarah and I played golf together in a number of tournaments. We went to a few charity balls, and I was sort of her date after my wife died."

JACQUE: *Sarah was a great cook. Uncle Ben loved her cheesecake. She was a real sweetheart, kind, gentle, loving. And we were quite close. Sarah used to say to me, about Valerie, "My sister is the meanest woman I've ever met!"*

After the Colonial tournament in 1992, Valerie controlled more and more of the daily details of Ben's life. For example, she refused to allow her husband to have his longtime favorite eggs and bacon for breakfast, nor would she let Ben order his dearly loved well-done steak at restaurants. She isolated him from the family and friends who would doubtless have made his declining years less lonely.

On June 11, 1994, Jacque married Robert Towery, forty-three years after they had graduated in the same class from Paschal High School. The ceremony was presided over by another high school classmate, Judge Dixon Holman, and it was held in the backyard of Jacque's son David and his wife Dayna. Following that event, Valerie rehired her cook, Willa May, and told Jacque she no longer needed to take her aunt and uncle to Shady Oaks for dinner.

JACQUE: *Shortly after my marriage to Robert, Valerie cut me off from seeing Uncle Ben. Every time I would call, she said he was asleep or too tired for visitors.*

In 1995, Ben was diagnosed with colon cancer. Valerie didn't believe the diagnosis, but after they sought a second opinion it was agreed that he should have surgery, followed by chemotherapy and radiation, as Royal had done several years earlier.

ROBERT: *One day, Uncle Ben was rushed to All Saints Hospital for emergency colon surgery. His condition was so acute that he must have been sick for some time, but no specialist had been consulted, and the doctor who performed the surgery was not a specialist. Jacque was in Harris Hospital across town.*

Jacque Hogan and Robert Towery
at their wedding—June 11, 1994
at the home of Jacque's son, Dr. David Corley.
JHT family collection.

While she was having a routine colonoscopy, the doctor had perforated Jacque's colon and she had to have surgery to repair the damage. I left Jacque and joined Valerie at All Saints while Ben had his emergency surgery. After her successful operation Jacque was released, and we went by to see her uncle at All Saints. This was the last time Jacque saw her Uncle Ben until the day before he died, in 1997. After Ben got out of the hospital, Jacque repeatedly called Valerie and asked if she could come see Ben. But Valerie always had some excuse why she shouldn't visit him. On several occasions Valerie told Jacque that because of his Alzheimer's he would not know her, and that would be disturbing to him. Valerie kept Jacque from seeing her beloved uncle for two years prior to his last visit to the hospital. As it turned out, after Ben's colon surgery, Valerie refused to take him for any more treatments. He never received the chemotherapy or radiation that would have prolonged his life. Dr. Jim Murphy told me that Valerie threw away all of the medications he had prescribed for Ben, and wouldn't let him do anything that might have made his life more pleasant. When we were talking, at one point, Dr. Murphy looked at me, paused, and finally said, "Valerie was a bitch."

Dr. Murphy recalled, "You know, in a sense Valerie was pretty paranoid, and she was very protective of Ben. I don't think there is any way that you can explain all of Valerie's activities or her mental aberrations. She constantly blamed me that I wasn't treating Ben the right way, but she wouldn't accept the fact that he had colon cancer. For several years, he showed signs of Alzheimer's, but she wouldn't accept that either. It was a very difficult situation."

By this time, Elizabeth Hudson was spending all of her time as Ben's caregiver, staying with him at home from the time he woke up until she went home for the evening. Elizabeth would occasionally drive him over to Shady Oaks, and the staff would call her when it was time for her to pick Ben up and take him home. Sometimes, just to get him out the house, Elizabeth would drive Ben around Fort Worth in his Cadillac.

Elizabeth said, "There were three things he really loved—and one of them was that car."

Marty Leonard recalled, "Ben would sneak out of the house and sit in his Cadillac and smoke. Valerie wouldn't let him smoke in the house. Over those final years, I felt like she restricted him from seeing people and doing some of the things he liked to do. But, to her way of thinking, she probably felt she was protecting him."

Ben's black Cadillac was always kept in pristine condition. Valerie would have people come over every weekend to wash, wax, and clean the interior of Ben's car. It was always full of gas and ready for Elizabeth to take Ben wherever he wished to go, but for the most part, that would only be the short drive to his beloved home away from home at Shady Oaks.

Elizabeth added, "Yes, there were three things he dearly loved. One was that car. The second was that club. He loved to go to that club—he didn't have to be around Mrs. Hogan. Gladys, their longtime housekeeper, told me that a few years before I came to work for the Hogans, Valerie had tired of Ben going to the club and told Gladys to ask Ben if he would stay home more. Gladys asked him, 'How come you don't stay at home with Mrs. Hogan more?' Mr. Hogan said, 'She is not pleasant.' Gladys told Mrs. Hogan that, and she retorted, 'Well, I'm just as pleasant as I can be. Aren't I Gladys?' Gladys couldn't say anything, she just shook her head."

In the late 1980s, while Ben could still drive, he would go out to the country to look for land on which to build a practice range with a short nine holes, or for a location for a new factory.

Elizabeth remembered, "One time, Mr. Hogan bought himself a ranch. He came home and told us, 'Well y'all, we got somewhere to go fishing now.' Later, from the other room, I overheard Mrs. Hogan say to him, 'Why did you go and buy a ranch? I'm not going to be able to take care of two houses! You go sell it!' He didn't have it more than two weeks. Mrs. Hogan's sister, Sarah, told me once, 'Everything has to be done her way. Valerie's always been that way.' And, I found that to be pretty true."

Elizabeth thought Ben was very sensitive to the fact that his employees lost jobs when the company was moved, and he thought maybe he could build another golf equipment plant to give them a place to work.

Elizabeth reflected, "That was the third thing—he loved that plant. He used to tell me all of the time that he hated that he sold it. He'd say to me, 'I have to build another one.'"

One day Elizabeth received a frantic call from Valerie that Ben was missing. Elizabeth threw her things together and rushed over to the Canterbury house. Jacque had received the same frantic call from Valerie and had arrived ahead of Elizabeth, as had the police. Valerie told the police that her husband was supposed to be at the club, but she had checked, and he wasn't there. She had driven over to Shady Oaks and saw that his car was gone. No one had seen him for several hours.

JACQUE: *Valerie was frantic. She was explaining everything to the police when the phone rang, and it was Shady Oaks letting us know that Ben was back at the club. Valerie and I got in my car and we drove over to Shady Oaks. We found Uncle Ben sitting at his table without a care in the world. When we asked him where he had been, he said matter-of-factly that he had driven out to Weatherford in search of some land to purchase. He said he knew where he was and he was fine.*

In December 1996, Jacque received a telephone call notifying her that her father had been admitted to Harris Methodist Hospital, that he was very ill, and wasn't expected to recover. For the next couple of weeks, Jacque would visit her father daily.

JACQUE: *One day, Tex Moncrief and Mel May, Daddy's longtime attorney, came up to his hospital room when I was there. I didn't know why they were there, but it felt like something was in the works. I left and told Daddy I had some things to do and would see him later. As it turned out, after I left they tried to get Daddy to give away some of his money. They knew he was dying and figured he should shield his money for tax purposes. But Daddy wasn't interested, and wanted to take it all with him. They explained that the government would get most of it, and given that ugly possibility, he finally gave in. He directed that each of his four grandchildren and I receive $10,000 each. I was surprised he included me, and I think it was his way of saying that he had finally forgiven me. I felt a sense of reconciliation.*

Jacque was holding her father's hand when Royal Hogan passed away on December 27, 1996. The funeral for Royal was at the chapel at Greenwood Funeral Home, and he was interred at the Greenwood Mausoleum in a crypt with his wife, Margaret, and their son,

Royal Dean Jr. They were in a separate section of the Mausoleum from the crypts of Princess and her husband Howard Ditto, and from another crypt where his mother Clara Williams Hogan was laid to rest.

JACQUE: *A little while after Daddy died, we were going though the office supply store to determine what to do with all of the furniture and supplies before we sold the building. In the safe, we found over $40,000 in cash. I always knew he kept some cash as a security blanket, a result of having lived through the Depression. But I had no idea he had that much in the safe.*

ROBERT: *When Ben was informed of his older brother's death, he told Elizabeth Hudson that he couldn't believe that 'Bubba was gone.' At this point, Elizabeth was very disturbed by the way Ben was being treated. She said that he simply didn't understand what was happening to him. He was not allowed to see old friends or even relatives, and he would ask her, "Where is everyone?" Valerie had asked Elizabeth not to pray with her husband, but when Valerie left the house, she and Ben would pray together.*

Ben was not a religious person, but he was very spiritual. And Royal's death made him even more isolated.

A few weeks after Royal's death, Jacque was informed that her father's will had stipulated skipping a generation, stating that outside of the $10,000 bequest, all assets would be divided among his grandchildren. However, before Royal's will was probated, Melvin May, who had been Royal's attorney, informed Jacque that another will existed--and that was Margaret Hogan's.

JACQUE: *When Daddy died in 1996, he left everything to his grandchildren, an event that I had anticipated because ever since I took the time off to meet Robert in San Antonio, my father had disowned me. Then, Mr. May called and told me my mother's will had been discovered and that it had stipulated, back in 1978, that Royal Dean Jr. and I would divide equally her share of one-half of my parents' assets. But, we never saw this will.*

Unfortunately, over the years since Margaret's death, Royal had comingled the assets from his wife's share of their estate that had been set up for Jacque and Royal Dean, so this created a legal quagmire, forcing the attorneys and the trust department at the bank to try and fairly arbitrate an equitable solution.

ROBERT: *Chuck Spence, the trust officer at NationsBank, brought in an outside attorney to mediate the dispute. The lawyer and bank made the decision to divide the entire estate left by Royal Hogan, half to Jacque and half to be split among his grandchildren. This situation was, in a way, the final demonstration of Royal's oversight and command over his daughter and his whole family—and this time it came from the grave.*

During the months following his brother's death, Ben was not doing very well. Valerie's lack of interest in medicines, treatments, even visits from the doctor had left Ben in a sad state of physical health. In spite of that decline, he would still rise every morning and dress completely.

Elizabeth recalled, "Every single day, Mr. Hogan put on all his clothes, suit pants, dress shirt, tie and shoes . . . everything. The day before he went to the hospital, I saw him after he had gotten out of bed, dressed completely, and walked out and sat down in his chair. We had a nice visit. The next morning, Valerie called me and said, 'Elizabeth, Mr. Hogan has gotten sick. I've already called Mr. Moncrief.' She said the ambulance was already on the way. She told me to come over—she needed me to be in the house. I drove over, and Mr. Hogan wasn't saying anything. He was just lying there. They put him in the ambulance, and Mrs. Hogan wanted to get in there with him, but they told her no, there was no room because they had to work on him while they drove him to the hospital. You know, he could have been suffering before, but he never said anything. He never complained. He never said he was in any pain."

The ambulance took Ben to All Saints Hospital while Tex Moncrief drove Valerie behind them. A little later in the day, Jacque received word that her uncle was in the hospital.

JACQUE: *The only reason I heard about it was a neighbor of my uncle's called his friend, who happened to be my bank trust officer, Chuck Spence, and told him an ambulance had taken Ben away. Thank God, Chuck called and told me. When I reached Uncle Ben's room at the hospital that evening, Valerie tried to prevent me from going in. She explained that he was not conscious and would not know me. I brushed her aside and went in to see my uncle. Valerie stayed in the other room of the suite. I went to the bed and said, "Uncle Ben, it's Jacqueline. I love you." The moment he saw me he rose up a little from the bed and called my name, "Jacqueline." I put my hand in his as I usually did, and he put his other hand on top of mine. Uncle Ben held my hand and looked at me with an expression that seemed to say, "Where have you been?" Tears came to my eyes, and I could not speak. I know that he would have asked Valerie about me in one of his more lucid times, and there is no telling what she told him about why I had not seen him in over two years. Looking back, I wish I had just driven over to their house and gone in to see him, regardless of what Valerie said or did. Every time I called she said he was not well enough to see anyone, and I believed and respected her response.*

The next morning, Valerie told the attending nurse that Ben was hungry, and sent her to get his breakfast. When the nurse returned to his room she found Valerie standing beside the bed, and then she realized Ben had passed away. The legendary Fort Worth golfer and "Favorite Son," William Ben Hogan, died on July 25, 1997, a short three weeks shy of his eighty-sixth birthday.

JACQUE: *When I learned that Ben had died, I called Byron Nelson and told him. It wasn't long before it hit the wire that Ben Hogan had passed away. Well, Valerie called and she was very mad at me, thinking I was the one who had leaked it to the press. When he was in the hospital, she didn't want anyone to know about it.*

ROBERT: *The condition in which Jacque found Ben that evening at the hospital did not jibe with the question he reportedly asked Valerie the next morning. "When am I going to get something to eat in here?" Of course, if he had improved considerably overnight, the question would be reasonable. In any event, Valerie sent the nurse or attendant who was with Ben to check on his breakfast. The attendant said that when she returned to his room, Ben had slipped away. That story may satisfy some people, but not me.*

In part because of the early episode involving Valerie and her baby sister Sarah, Robert remained suspicious about the circumstances

University Christian Church, where the memorial service for Ben Hogan was held.
Photo by Peter Barbour.

of Ben's death.

When the day came for Ben's funeral, Jacque had been told she and her husband should be at Valerie's to drive to the memorial service with everyone in a limo, so Robert and Jacque drove over to their home. Valerie's grandniece and grandnephew were there, and they got into a limo with Marty Leonard and Evelyn Dickey, a very good friend of Valerie's. Jacque and Robert went to the church in a separate limo.

JACQUE: *The service was at University Christian Church, and we sat on the second row. We greeted a lot of people we knew, some of them good friends of ours. The reception following the funeral was held at Shady Oaks Country Club. We were visiting with friends like Ben Crenshaw and others. After a short period, we received a message that Valerie wanted "the Hogans" to go downstairs. That seemed like a strange request, but we decided to comply, since we didn't want to offend Valerie on that particular day. So, as the closest blood relative of Ben Hogan, I was denied the opportunity of visiting with friends and acquaintances of my uncle's. It was disgraceful. We were relegated to the downstairs, and if we hadn't been in a limo with other people, I would have left right away.*

After the day of the funeral, Jacque had only one other occasion to talk to Valerie before she died in 1999. Valerie had called and left a message on Jacque's answering machine to return the call.

JACQUE: *When I called Valerie back, she said that she had heard that I was spreading some sort of rumor and she was upset. I asked what the rumor was. Valerie said, "Never mind, I found out it wasn't you." Then she hung up.*

Valerie Fox Hogan remained an enigma to the end. From the time of his near-fatal accident in 1949 until Ben's death, Valerie had attempted to protect her husband's legacy. The end result was that family and friends were completely shut out of Ben's life.

Jacque likes to remember her uncle from earlier times, when he was dominating the game of golf. In 1947, Ben was the defending champion at the Colonial NIT. At that time, there were no ropes separating the gallery from the golfers, but Jacque was well-schooled by her father in the rules of golf etiquette.

JACQUE: *Growing up, I was always told by my daddy, "You do not ever speak to any golfers on the course, especially your uncle."*

During the second round of the 1947 tournament, fourteen-year-old Jacqueline

FACING PAGE: Tribute honoring the late Ben Hogan, written by Marty Leonard for the Shady Oaks Country Club newsletter, the *Oak Leaf*, August 1997. Courtesy of Marty Leonard.

We have lost the man, Ben Hogan. But we will never lose the spirit of Ben Hogan. Shady Oaks was a special place, a refuge to Ben in his retirement years and before.
And his presence there not only gave SOCC a prominent place in the golf world, but it also gave the members, guests, and staff the chance to know, respect, admire, and love a golfing legend. Each of us has an image and our own special memories of Ben, or Mr. Hogan. So I hope the following thoughts will jog your own memories and make you smile when thinking of Ben Hogan.

First, I cannot think of Ben without thinking of Valerie, his wife and lifelong companion of 62 years. How often we saw them together having lunch or dinner. Personally, I always loved the way he said "Valerie." He made it sound different than anyone else.

We think of:

- *His hours of practice on the Little Nine with many a young man never having to step away from his shag bag to retrieve his precise shots.*
- *His powerful and masterful hands.*
- *His dress hat—felt in winter and straw in summer.*
- *His desire and drive for perfection.*
- *His black Cadillac.*
- *The white Hogan cap.*
- *His distinctive walk.*
- *Max, man's and Ben's best friend.*
- *And Buster.*
- *His place at the corner table.*
- *His honesty and direct approach.*
- *The extra spike on his cordovan shoe.*
- *His best friend, Marvin.*
- *Walking the course to get his exercise, with club.*
- *Introducing himself as Henny Bogan.*
- *Always a gentleman.*
- *The course record.*
- *The way he preferred his bag to be slanted on the cart.*
- *The sincerity of his greetings.*
- *A little fade.*
- *The sound of his golf shots.*
- *The swing game.*
- *Gin rummy.*
- *The Hogan Company and excellence in club design.*
- *And many more. . . .*

I thank God for the life of Ben. He and our memories of him will live forever, but especially for us at Shady Oaks.

MARTY LEONARD

P. S. I resisted including my many longtime personal memories of Ben—not enough space in the entire newsletter!

was walking down the middle of the fourteenth fairway at Colonial when out of the corner of her eye, she saw her uncle walking toward his ball and approaching her.

JACQUE: *I saw Uncle Ben coming up, so I just kept walking. As he passed me, he turned and said, "Oh, hello Jacqueline. How are you?' Taking a deep breath, I said, "I'm just fine Uncle Ben." I was scared to death I might get into trouble because I wasn't supposed to speak to him. Nevertheless, I always found it fascinating that he spoke to me. For the entirety of Uncle Ben's career, he was famous for saying only two words . . . while playing in a professional tournament. When he reached the green, he was known to turn to his fellow competitor and say, "You're out."*

Jacque's most lasting image of her dad and uncle together involved a time when they were in their prime. Jacque's father took her and her mom to Chicago in June of 1942. They stayed at the elegant Edgewater Beach Hotel on the shores of Lake Michigan. For four glorious days they followed Ben at the Ridgemoor Country Club, playing in the Hale America Open. She has said she'll never forget the final round, watching her beloved Uncle Ben, leading by three strokes, walking up to the eighteenth hole. His playing companion was the legendary Bobby Jones. Jacque had often heard her father and uncle tell stories about Bobby Jones's accomplishments and his 1929 ticker-tape parade in New York City.

JACQUE: *I remember it so well. The best time of that trip was when I went to Don the Beachcomber with Daddy, Mother, Uncle Ben, and Valerie to celebrate Uncle Ben's victory in Chicago. I'll never forget the feelings of admiration from others in the room for my uncle. I remember looking at my dad and seeing an expression of complete pride in his younger brother. One of my most lasting images of them is when Uncle Ben took out the USGA Open Medallion he had been awarded earlier that day and held it up for my dad to admire as Dad patted Uncle Ben on the shoulder and beamed. They were wonderful companions in their journey in life, always supportive of each other, dedicated to their beliefs, professional to the end, and the best of brothers.*

The Brothers Hogan is from start to finish an American story. It embraces the family perspective and highlights the obstacles and hardships the two brothers overcame as they diligently worked their way to success in their individual careers. This book was never intended to portray the brothers, or their extended family, to be any better or worse than they were in day-to-day life. But much of their extraordinary story has been ignored over the years, and it needed telling. In the end, it can only be hoped that the reader has found *The Brothers Hogan* to be an insightful story of two incredible brothers who helped put Fort Worth on the map in the great state of Texas. Royal and Ben Hogan were not perfect, but both rose from humble beginnings to remarkable levels of achievement, wealth, and recognition. Through his vigilant, unbending work ethic and business savvy, Royal left his stamp on the larger business community, at the same time that he became a champion in the world of amateur golf. Ben Hogan, through his steely practice regimens, intellectual applications to the professional game, and his unwavering courage in the face of adversity, left incredible records in the archives of professional golf that were destined to be known around the world.

Their legacy seems perfectly captured in one young girl's memory of the smiling faces of two brothers, basking in a golden moment when they were both on top of the world.

HOGAN FAMILY ANCESTRY

JACQUELINE HOGAN TOWERY IS THE last of her family to be known by the name of Hogan. Jacque's only sibling was her younger brother, Royal Dean Hogan Jr., who died too young, before he ever had any children. Jacque's father, Royal, had an older sister, Princess, who married H. Howard Ditto and remained childless. Royal's younger brother Ben and his wife never had any offspring.

Jacque's late husband, Robert Towery, who started research on this book back in 1998, was consumed with his thirst for Hogan family history and ancestral lines. Robert began his quest for the truth concerning the family legacy by gathering family information and contemplating the process. In his notes, we found the following:

Do you know anything about your family ancestry? Do your children know as much as you know? Have you written down your ancestry for future generations? If you haven't already started, please begin now.

Far too often we think of the immediate family with some thought given to our grandfathers, grandmothers, uncles, aunts, and cousins. But how much do we think about the greater extended family, like our great- and great-great grandparents, or our great- and great-great uncles and aunts, and all of their children?

It is not easy when all of your ancestors are deceased. Finding stories about their childhood years is next to impossible. That is why I encourage you to start now and keep at it. Your children and their children and those who follow deserve your effort.

JACQUE: *Over a period of several years, Robert tirelessly researched the genealogy of my mother, who was born Margaret Lenora*

Duncan, and my father, Royal Dean Hogan. He was able to discover a wealth of information on five generations of my daddy's family, but could find very little on the four generations on my mother's side.

ELIJAH K. HOGAN

ROBERT: *Jacque's paternal great-great grandfather was Elijah K. Hogan. He was a blacksmith, as was her great grandfather Alex Hogan and her grandfather Chester Hogan. Jacque was told that Elijah's wife was named Martha and that the best information they had indicated she was born in Kentucky.*

Elijah Hogan was born around 1828 in North Carolina, the home state of his parents. His wife's first name was Martha, but there was no recollection or written proof of her maiden name. Elijah and Martha had four children, all born in Choctaw County, Mississippi. Their children were William Alexander "Alex", Mary, Margaret, and John.

WILLIAM ALEXANDER "Alex" HOGAN

"Alex" Hogan was born on May 16, 1848. When Alex was sixteen years of age, he enlisted in the First Mississippi Cavalry Reserves, where he enhanced his skills as a blacksmith, the trade of his father. After the Civil War ended, Alex married Cynthia Ann Tennyson, the daughter of John Washington Tennyson of Kentucky, and Ann Biggers Tennyson, from South Carolina. Cynthia was born in Mississippi on December 13, 1843, and was four and one-half years older than Alex. The many Hogan children started arriving in 1865, and by early 1876 there were five, all born in Choctaw County, Mississippi: William (1865), Josephine (1866), Martha (1868), Mary Emmaline (1870), and David Ephraim (1876).

ROBERT: *Alex and his family left Mississippi around 1877 and traveled about seven hundred miles to their new home in Texas. They settled in Dublin, because it was largely a farming community. The town was still relatively new and undeveloped when the Hogans arrived.*

The Hogans' next three children were born in Dublin: Ella in 1878, then Gaston Barbee in 1881, and Oscar Silas Charles in early 1883.

JACQUE: *My grandfather, Chester, arrived in the Hogan family on February 3, 1885. Unfortunately, I never knew him. He was born in Roby, Texas, in Fisher County, about 160 miles northwest of Dublin. I have found no explanation as to why my grandfather was born in Roby. He was the ninth child of Alex and Cynthia, and a tenth child, Floyd Hogan, was born in Dripping Springs, Texas, in 1886. Several articles and books have*

Alex and Cynthia Hogan with four of their ten children, one of whom was Chester Hogan.
JHT family collection..

and his time in the cavalry, and he opened a blacksmith shop on Elm Street.

CHESTER HOGAN

ROBERT: *We do not have much information about Chester's childhood, but he seemed to be a rather quiet, pleasant child who didn't develop a lot of close relationships. He was physically strong, especially in his arms and large hands, which was an asset in the family trade of blacksmithing.*

Once Chester was old enough, he joined his father in the trade, and the shop eventually bore Chester's name. In a largely farming community, a blacksmith shop was essential, and the work involved repairing wagons, plows, and tools; shoeing horses; and occasionally making or converting harnesses. The Hogans were not getting rich with all this hard work, but it provided a decent living for the family.

JACQUE: *My father and Uncle Ben always believed that it was the tough times in their early lives that made them strive so hard for success. Uncle Ben once said to me, "I feel sorry for rich kids. I really do, because they are never going to have the opportunity I had. I had tough days all my life, and I learned to handle them. . . . Every day that I progressed was a joy to me, and I recognized that fact every single morning. I don't think I would have done what I've done if I hadn't had the*

stated that Chester was one of 'only' eight children, but Robert's research found the other two siblings.

When Alex and Cynthia arrived in Dublin with their family, one of the first things they did was to join the First Baptist Church. Having a home church was always part of the Hogan family. Alex abandoned farming in favor of the trade he learned from his father

Chester Hogan, bent over, shoes a horse as his
two assistants help out.
JHT family collection..

*tough days to begin with." And, it should be
no surprise that my daddy felt much the same
way.*

For a while, as a teenager, Chester worked
in Dublin's Dr. Pepper Bottling Company,
washing bottles that had been returned to
the plant. The company then refilled, corked,
and crated the bottles for subsequent ship-
ments to dealer outlets. Before long, though,
he joined his father at the blacksmith shop
and learned his future trade. Being a blacksmith in those days was an honorable trade,
and Alex and Chester were kept busy with
the work created by the harsh demands of

Alex and Cynthia Hogan were distributors
for Watkins Remedies.
JHT family collection.

running a farm. However, once farming began to lose its appeal as a means of making a living, the blacksmith business fell off. Alex and Cynthia Hogan supplemented their meager income by selling Watkins Remedies from their two-horse-drawn carriage. Chester took over the blacksmith shop, and continued working with his father when Alex wasn't peddling the "remedies." Chester was a man of good character, but he suffered from periods of depression, which doctors later termed "melancholy."

Chester's mother, Cynthia, died June 30, 1907, but his father outlived Chester, passing away on March 11, 1936. Both are buried in the Old Dublin Memorial Park in Dublin, along with their son Chester.

CLARA WILLIAMS HOGAN ("MAMA" HOGAN)

Clara Williams Hogan, known to all during her adult life as Mama Hogan, was Jacque's paternal grandmother. In today's terms, Mama Hogan would probably be known as a "control freak," or as someone suffering from obsessive-compulsive disorder. However, she was the person most responsible for the disciplined determination and eventual success of her three children, Princess, Royal, and Ben. Much like her future husband, Chester, Clara was born in Texas to a family that had migrated from other parts of the South.

THE WILLIAMS FAMILY GENEALOGY

ROBERT: *Clara's paternal grandfather, Benjamin Claude Williams, was born in North Carolina around 1824 and died in August of 1875. Her paternal grandmother, Sophronia Pope Williams, was born around 1819, but I could not find out where. She was five to six years older than her husband, which was not uncommon in those days. They were married December 3, 1845, and moved west to Delhi, Richland Parish, Louisiana, where they started a family.*

Clara's father, Benjamin Hicks Williams, and her mother, Lelia Prentiss Motley Williams, were both born in Delhi, Richland Parish, Louisiana, in 1855 and 1862, respectively.

Benjamin and Lelia eventually moved to Texas where Mama Hogan, Clara Saphronia Williams, was born on March 14, 1890, in Comanche, Texas, twenty-one miles southwest of Dublin. The Williams family lived in a rented house on Grafton Street in Dublin, just a few blocks from the Hogan blacksmith shop. Clara's father was a cotton buyer who graded bales of raw cotton fiber and processed them for shipment to northern clothing- and thread-manufacturing companies. He died July 8, 1936, in Fort Worth, and is buried in the Old Dublin Memorial Park.

Chester married Clara Saphronia Williams on July 31, 1906. After their ceremony, Clara and Chester lived in a small square bungalow at 503 North Camden, on the corner of Camden and East Harris Street in Dublin. This is where two of their three children were born with the exception of Ben, who was born in nearby Stephenville for reasons unclear in the family history. The children all grew up in Dublin until Clara moved the family to Fort Worth in 1921.

JACQUE: *My husband, Robert, once told me that he wished he had known Clara. He said, "She seemed to be so much like my mother—strong in character, committed in loyalty, and supportive of 'her boys' to a fault."*

Princess, Ben, and Royal with their bikes.
JHT family collection.

HARRY AND MYRTLE DUNCAN

ROBERT: *The paternal grandfather of Jacque's mother, Margaret Lenora Duncan, was H. M. Duncan. He lived in the Fort Worth area and passed away in 1933. Nothing is known of his family roots or the whereabouts of their origins. I did discover that his wife was named Henrietta, and she was born in 1861. She passed eleven years before her husband, in 1922.*

JACQUE: *Robert was very disappointed he could not find more information on my mother's side of the family. He told me it was sad that families just didn't keep records, and without knowing the origins of my family it was very difficult to search for any information about their lives.*

H. M. Duncan and his wife Henrietta had a son, Harry M. Duncan, who married Myrtle "BB" Chrisman in Fort Worth, soon after the turn of the twentieth century. Myrtle's parents, James Chrisman and Celia Bobo Chrisman, had settled in Fort Worth in the early 1880s, and Myrtle was born there in 1888.

Harry's accident at Hogan Office Supply on Main Street took his life on July 3, 1953. Myrtle lived to be eighty years old, dying on December 16, 1968.

Royal Hogan draws his toy pistol, with Ben on the hobbyhorse and Princess under her parasol. JHT family collection.

On June 24, 1909, Harry and Myrtle's daughter, Margaret Lenora Duncan, was born in Fort Worth. Margaret would eventually meet and marry Royal Hogan in 1925, and they had two children: Jacqueline in 1933 and Royal Dean Hogan Jr. in 1948.

BIBLIOGRAPHY

BOOKS:

Buenger, Victoria and Walter L. Texas
Merchant: Marvin Leonard and Fort Worth. College
Station: Texas A&M University Press, 2008.

Demeret, Jimmy. *My Partner, Ben Hogan*.
London: Peter Davies, 1954.

Roberson, Dennis. *Colonial: 60 Years of Greatness*.
Fort Worth: Panache Partners, 2006.

Towle, Mike. I *Remember Ben Hogan*.
Nashville: Cumberland House, 2000.

Trimble, Frances G. *Colonial Country Club:
Diamond Jubilee Celebration–75 Years*.
Fort Worth: Colonial Country Club, 2010.

Tschetter, Kris. *Mr. Hogan, The Man I Knew*.
New York: Gotham Books, 2010.

Willitt, Sue Van Noy. *The Waldemar Story:
Camping in Texas Hill Country*.
Austin, Texas: Eakin Press, 1998.

NEWSPAPERS:

Bill Rives, "Fort Worth Dignitaries Greet
Hogan," *Dallas Morning News*, July 15, 1953.

Scott Thurber, "Ben Hogan Out of Danger After
Surgery," *El Paso Times*, March 4, 1949.

"Ben Hogan in 'Fair' Condition at Texas Hospital
After Collision," *New York Times*, February 3, 1949.

INTERNET:

White, Jack. "The Way We Were—Architecture in
Fort Worth," (September 3, 2011). http://www.fort-
wortharchitecture.com/oldftw/oldftw.htm.

"History of the Club," Thunderbird Country Club,
Rancho Mirage, California (2012). http://www.thun-
derbirdcc.org.

"Timeline: Ben Hogan Company." Fort Worth
Star-Telegram (October 25, 1999). http://www.
star-telegram.com.

"History and Tradition," Fort Worth Stock Show
and Rodeo (October 24, 2013). http://www.fwssr.
com.

"History of the Hogan Company" (2002; site
removed 2006). http://www.benhogan.com.

INDEX